Healing Health Anxiety

The Comprehensive Guide

Laura Abate

TEACH Services, Inc.
PUBLISHING
www.TEACHServices.com • (800) 367-1844

World rights reserved. This book or any portion thereof may not be copied or reproduced in any form or manner whatever, except as provided by law, without the written permission of the publisher, except by a reviewer who may quote brief passages in a review.

The author assumes full responsibility for the accuracy of all facts and quotations as cited in this book. The opinions expressed in this book are the author's personal views and interpretations, and do not necessarily reflect those of the publisher.

This book is provided with the understanding that the publisher is not engaged in giving spiritual, legal, medical, or other professional advice. If authoritative advice is needed, the reader should seek the counsel of a competent professional.

Copyright © 2017 Laura Abate

Copyright © 2017 TEACH Services, Inc.

ISBN-13: 978-1-4796-0715-0 (Paperback)

ISBN-13: 978-1-4796-0716-7 (ePub)

ISBN-13: 978-1-4796-0717-4 (Mobi)

Library of Congress Control Number: 2016920887

To all who suffer from health anxiety,

I am with you.

Table of Contents

As It Began 7
Introduction 10
Chapter One: Anxiety Neurophysiology 17
Chapter Two: Brain Care 28
Chapter Three: Mind Care 64
Chapter 4: Spirit Care 99
References 125
Index 131

As It Began

I love understanding the body and mind. When listening to people share about their health, I gather a sense of their mind-body expression and then reflect this impression back to them. I want each person to love and cherish his or her body as much as I love mine. One of my dearest prayers is to give thanks for each organ and function. Sight! Hearing! Dancing!

The body is precious and fascinating to me. As a small child, I remember gazing at my hand in the morning sunlight streaming through the window, awestruck by this little appendage moving about. Soon after, I began ballet, and I loved to twirl, point my toes, and take little leaps. Yet, a few years later, I began to experience my mind-body as a highly reactive and sensitive entity capable of causing unpredictable pain and misery. My mind-body now seemed to be a magnet for abdominal discomfort or terror of losing my mother when she would simply go out for the evening. Not knowing that the standard American diet (SAD) that I consumed as a child was a culprit in causing these baffling paroxysms of torment, I would go to bed at night apprehensive, fearing another episode of intense nausea and dreadful vomiting. I learned later that the high animal fat and protein as well as the dairy and processed foodless food that was served at home on a daily basis were partly responsible in causing my fears.

Years later, a high school physiology class gave me the conviction that the body is the most interesting biology there is. It wasn't until that physiology class that I felt the inspiration to seek further understanding of the workings and mysteries of my body; if I had great knowledge of physiology, then maybe I could understand my body and be able to lessen the strange discomforts that it would manifest.

I couldn't get that knowledge fast enough.

Just before turning twenty, I began to experience attacks of de-realization, inner ear disequilibrium and bewildering fear shocks that suddenly came out of nowhere. Feeling out of control and helpless, I contemplated ending my life as the only way to stop the overwhelming mental agony. Bewildered and terrified of these baffling, mysterious attacks that had no name or correlation, I assumed that they were caused by a brain tumor wedged deep into my brain. A physician gave me a tranquilizer, and a social worker stated I was going through an identity crisis. After some time, I learned these spontaneous attacks were none other than simple but hideous panic attacks. They faded after a few months, and left me alone for several years.

Learning about various diseases in nursing school provoked further fear as I wondered if I had—yes, I did feel light headed, had headaches, was clumsy and nauseous. I saw these effects in multiple sclerosis or, again, due to a brain tumor. My body was wildly reactive—to what I didn't know—with fear and light-headedness happening all too randomly. Alcohol made me violently ill, caffeine made me nervous, and the little amount of marijuana I tried resulted in agonizing, protracted panic attacks. *To heck with these awful joints*, I thought.

Through the years, physical manifestations became seemingly more bizarre. Irritable bowel syndrome, spontaneous hemorrhagic throat rupturing, migraines, systemic itching, and out-of-control foodless food bingeing were just a few of the situations I faced. The nagging possibility of now being struck with something fatal became an intractable haunting as familiar or new sensations were experienced leaving me baffled. Sensations veered into automatic processing of pending catastrophe: "It could happen to me! Maybe! What if?" The rut of catastrophic thinking now cut a deep and enduring furrow into my brain, sinking me deeper into the calamitous ditch.

I found my thoughts and feelings to be highly reactive as well. Blissfully in love or raging at injustice, my feelings were rich and alive. I would agonize about unpredictable or chronic suffering that could strike any sentient being including myself. "Why?" I asked as a child, "am I having all this pain? Is this what human existence on earth is going to be about? I don't think I like being a human or being here in this scary world." After hearing stories of people, including children, getting sick and sometimes dying, I despaired for them and began to ask: "Why not me? The horror of this unfairness! It could happen to me as well. Maybe! What if?"

One day, I asked my mother what caused these terrible diseases, and she replied, "We don't know." The hollowness of her answer haunted me. *What hope can there be then?* I wondered. I felt trapped in a merciless and unpredictable world. I did not yet know that I would grow up to learn why these terrible diseases struck and how to stay safe, thriving and radiant in life, free from disease.

I was brought up in a religious home where any contemplation of spirituality was squelched while family abuse overwhelmed and violated my sense of reality and search for God. Furthermore, science seemed calmly superior to religion, which appeared myth-like and disturbing. I learned that people with terminal illnesses were freezing themselves near death to try to resume life in the future when a cure for that disease would hopefully be found. Did their souls go to heaven for that time interval and then return? How about from hell? Preposterous! People would preach about the horror of hell as well as the unthinkable agony of the crucifixion and God's Son having to be tortured as a sacrifice for us. Why did that unspeakable horror happen? Torture, blood, burnings—I found no redeeming value within these teachings, and I was baffled and horrified that people could espouse such black misery as the basis of their spirituality.

However, one Sunday school class I attended had us watch a movie about Jesus, and I felt a wave of serenity and sweet rich love envelope my being as I watched this beautiful Man and felt His presence beside me, lifting me above squalor, comforting me as no one had ever done. There *was* a safe and beautiful presence, despite the mechanics, mundanity, random terrifying events, and violent hypocrisy of life as I had so far found it. A seed was then planted to grow into a resilient tree, standing up to the despair and exhaustion of struggling with pain and health anxiety. I was given gifts of endurance and intuition that kept me from succumbing to the struggles of terror and anguish and allowed me to embrace life, nursing, and then true healing. Although it seemed intent on crippling me forever, fear never destroyed me.

Although it seemed intent on crippling me forever, fear never destroyed me.

Introduction

Health anxiety is a fear-based preoccupation with one's health that is triggered by somatic sensations and perceptions. Health anxiety is fear of the possibility of having or getting a serious illness with heightened sensitivity towards minor bodily symptoms and functions. Temporary or little reassurance is gained from medical consultations that show no clinical abnormalities. One fears that a serious disease is now manifesting despite relative and/or baseline wellness. Health anxiety is a problem of worry and fear, not health. Yet, because of heightened sensitivities that many bodies possess, health anxiety will convince you that the problem IS your health. But I say again, health anxiety is a problem of worry and fear, not health.

Health anxiety is a problem of worry and fear, not health.

Millions of people struggle with health anxiety throughout the world independent of race, gender, or class. Anxiety disorders affect 28 percent of Americans and tend to run in families. It is estimated that between 3 percent to 8 percent of Americans suffer from health anxiety. Health anxiety can begin at any age with the most common onset in early adulthood, and it is equally common in males and females. Anxiety disorders are multifaceted: progressive (gets worse), acute (sudden attacks), chronic (going on and on intermittently), and prevalent (you aren't the only one to have this). Still, those with anxiety are not doomed; while those who experience chronic, progressive, and prevalent forms of anxiety will never lose their heightened physical sensitivity and hypervigilant alarm system, they can learn to manage anxiety and live in recovery. Famous people who struggled with health anxiety include Florence Nightingale (mother of modern nursing), Charles Darwin (biologist who formulated the theory of evolution), Alfred Lord Tennyson (poet laureate of Great Britain during Queen Victoria's reign), Howard Hughes (business tycoon), and Immanuel Kant (philosopher). Even Hitler, leader of Nazi Germany who initiated World War II and fascism, was preoccupied with somatic anxiety, mostly abdominal and throat concerns.

Health anxiety or illness anxiety disorder (the older term hypochondriasis, meaning below the ribs, where it was thought to originate, is no longer used) is classified under the Somatic Symptom and Related Disorders category according to the Diagnostic Statistical Manual, 5th edition (DSM-V, 2013), the basic psychiatric textbook of the American Psychiatric Association. Somatic symptom and related disorders also include: somatic symptom disorder (persistently high levels of anxiety about genuine somatic symptoms having no medical basis. Physical complaints commonly revolve around gastrointestinal, neurological, reproductive, and pain symptoms), conversion disorder or functional neurological symptom disorder (i.e. an arm becomes paralyzed without a medical cause and is understood as psychic stress converted into neurologic somatic manifestations), factitious disorder (using deception to appear physically or mentally ill in self or another without seeking external benefits, unlike malingering) and psychiatric factors affecting other medical conditions (emotions and behaviors having a negative effect on a medical condition as in rage episodes exacerbating asthma).

Let us ask for a moment: what is the rotational axis that health anxiety turns on? Is it a death phobia, post health trauma hypersensitivity, or a simple anxiety disorder with fear of disease as the focus? For example, the philosopher Immanuel Kant (1724–1804) had a congenital skeletal defect that caused him to develop an abnormally small chest, which compressed his heart and lungs, creating a delicate constitution and health anxiety anguish.

My health anxiety took off exponentially when one evening clearing my throat, it burst into unstoppable gushing blood. This went on intermittently for ten years. A friend and nurse I worked with after seeing me hemorrhage one day told me she would have been terrified if the same thing had happened to her. Well, of course, as this is an example of gut-wrenching fear provoked by a sudden eruption of something that appears to be dangerous. Nearly everyone can relate. We can use this alarming and somatic event to differentiate fear, anxiety, phobia, and obsession: fearing return of more bloody throat attacks would be anxiety while the dread of anything throat related i.e. swallowing pills, dryness, congestion, and coughing would be a phobia. Persistent and intrusive thoughts of a bleeding throat would be a symptom of obsessive-compulsive disorder.

Health anxiety is not a character flaw like being prone to hysteria, weakness, selfishness, or laziness. Still, experiencing the shame, bafflement, and embarrassment of this disorder is hard to avoid. Although health anxiety is challenging to manage, let us begin to understand its mechanics, which is integral to recovery and healing.

Fundamentally, health anxiety is neurology gone bad, resulting in genuine somatic discomfort and dysfunction with excessive fear and concern regarding these manifestations. How does this dysfunctional neurological pattern come to be? It is a combination of a genetically-based, highly sensitive fear center in the brain called the amygdala as well as a toxic state of mind and body engendering catastrophic interpretation of pain and somatic manifestations. Life events can contribute to health anxiety: major disease outbreaks or predicted pandemics, experiencing health trauma of self or a loved one, or a chronically poor lifestyle with excessive body toxicity (i.e. the ubiquitous standard American diet). Medical issues as fibromyalgia or thyroid disturbances can precipitate attacks of health anxiety. Struggles to find meaning and/or fear of death and other spiritual maladies can play a part as health anxiety can drag on seemingly endlessly. Yet, the main culprit in health anxiety is how one thinks about his or her health with corresponding thinking errors and intolerance of uncertainty.

Through a feedback system, health anxiety fortifies itself with propaganda both internal, such as "This cramp! Isn't this what Aunt Betty had that turned out to be a melon sized abdominal tumor?", and external, like being told, "Abdominal cramping can be a sign of colon cancer and should be investigated promptly with a medical examination and colonoscopy. Please bring your insurance card for your appointment and arrive early to fill out pages and pages of forms." Both types of propaganda utilize the thinking error of catastrophic interpretation and fear tactics to funnel would-be patients into the medical system as the ultimate avenue to treat any malady of body or mind. Let's know right now that the third cause of death in the United States is medical error: medication side effects and medical interventions gone bad. So whoa Nelly, before you slide down that funnel, consider that the medical system is not the ultimate answer or healing method to reflexively pursue in all healthcare situations.

Health anxiety is progressive as it aims to maintain preoccupation with health fear while driving thinking in a negative and extreme direction. It also tends to worsen with age. Now, just because someone is healthy does not mean they will be free of health anxiety. Just because someone is unhealthy or ill does not mean they will suffer from health anxiety. There are those who smoke and have health anxiety and those who do not smoke yet still have health anxiety. The mystery of those who suffer from health anxiety despite being blessed with good health while another has little concern and is practically at death's doorstop points to the fascination of the human being. Left untreated, health anxiety will continue to loom and confound mental health, contributing to the work the body must do around the clock.

Many people with health anxiety have sensitive and/or volatile bodies that react to various internal and external stimuli with uncomfortable and disconcerting manifestations, affecting the body anywhere from the head down to the toes: congestion, aches, fatigue, shooting pains, spasms, lightheadedness, baffling numbness, exploding diarrhea coming on suddenly and then gone. Or perhaps we struggle with benign yet consuming conditions such as fibromyalgia, chronic fatigue, iliocecal valve syndrome, and candidiasis or food intolerances. One feels plagued with an unstable and frightening relationship with one's body when perplexing and unpleasant manifestations occur unpredictably all too often without warning or reason.

Furthermore, physical signs and sensations can be expressions of unresolved conflicts related to anxiety, frustration, anger, depression, and guilt, offering proof of the mind-body link. This link can involve channeling mental distress into sensations engendering the vicious circle of sensations-anxiety-sensations-anxiety. These conditions confound health anxiety while many health professionals are unlikely to treat these controversial and benign but very real disorders. We fearfully overreact towards our heightened sensations, interpreting them catastrophically as a worst-case scenario flashes before our minds: "Wait! This is that same throat soreness I had last year that just went away, but this time I coughed three times in two minutes! Maybe now it's something serious! What if?"

When seeking care for the somatic concerns connected with health anxiety, treatment merges between two camps: psychotherapy and medical intervention. However, neither camp wants to step on the other camp's toes. The medical system is a powerful and massive technology with large toes. As we are taught to eat pieces of a cadaver and processed foodless food combined with alien breast milk to drink, we are also taught to automatically go to the doctor as the ultimate expert regarding any malady real or not. This is part of the modern-day mentality and push button technology, where profits flourish when people abandon responsibility for their health and show up to sit on the examining table.

"I didn't go to medical school," people say. "Fix me please, Doctor." Physicians are trained to diagnose and medicate recognized pathology, yet much of pathology is covert and/or stems from body-mind conflicts. Lab results may be normal, but they cannot rectify the underlying misery of catastrophic thinking, which stems from mysterious bodily sensations and observations. The expertise and practice of any physician lies on a continuum from insensitive clinicians practicing recipe medicine to greatly knowledgeable, ethical, and caring medical doctors. Why give a doctor who may be preoccupied with a financial interest in billing your insurance company control over your life and future? Reflexively accepting another's word regarding your health weakens your healing skills; consulting with a professional needs to be in partnership with the doctor as health and healing is everyone's responsibility. However, some doctors will back away when faced with an anxious and "somatic" patient. It just ain't their bag. The good news is that there are other alternatives to seeing medical professionals.

Psychotherapy will easily take on any major or minor mental malady: anxiety, depression, addiction, personality disorders, psychotic disorders, and just about everything else listed in the DSM-V. But psychotherapy becomes a little uneasy when a patient expresses a concern about some strange physical manifestation. Any other fear in things such as bridges, people, or insects is addressed confidently, but this confidence is not seen when it concerns the body. Psychotherapy usually refers somatic concerns to the medical realm, which can heighten fear of the unknown as the patient is sent to another professional: "Is something seriously wrong with me? Maybe, what if?" If the medical camp finds no pathology, a green light is given to the therapist to see this problem as a cognitive-behavioral problem. However, there still needs to be a plan of care for a highly sensitive body. Which camp will address that need?

There is another little camp involved: the spiritual camp, which medicine backs away from and psychology will tip its hat towards. Many spiritual paths embrace energy healing and believe that prayer is powerful enough to heal any physical and/or psychological problem. Several Christian scientists affirm that illness results from negative health thoughts and to avoid medical treatment except dental care, which is acceptable. Other faith healers affirm that faith in God will prevent or cure illness and that illness is the result of a spiritual malady. Each camp reaches its limit of what it can offer the sufferer that can leave the "hypochondriac" as a contemptuous and piteous joke; the mystery of the mind-body-spirit connection lurks while the sufferer feels helpless and out of control. Only a three-fold camp will offer healing: caring for the body and brain, healthy thinking, and spiritual fitness.

> *Only a three-fold camp will offer healing: caring for the body and brain, healthy thinking, and spiritual fitness.*

Having an inner sense of spiritual/intuitive grace that is receptive to something beyond the concrete and mechanical responses to life not only helps to decrease involvement within the medical-psychiatric system but also liberates the mind from catastrophic obsession and into full living. This is what we were born to do. Healing from health anxiety regains awareness of a spiritual energy flow that gives guidance on how to care for your body, mind, and soul. New thinking pathways are created, granting the freedom to consult with your greater Healer, and when needed, a trusted healthcare practitioner.

For some, there may be a secondary benefit from having an anxiety disorder such as gaining attention, providing rationalization ("I can't work because of this anxiety disorder"), or fortifying a victim mentality. These hidden agendas will impede healing and must be recognized and rooted out. The pain of this disorder must be stronger than any gain received in order for motivation towards healing to ensue. Some individuals with anxiety disorders will obtain short term "relief" with drugs. Others will have their lives shortened from the agony of this illness, and a few will go to any lengths to obtain healing, as in changing one's diet and/or finding a relationship with God.

Although health anxiety can be baffling and complicated, it can be treated. Thinking and behavioral skills can be learned to manage destructive health anxiety and to free yourself into the life you are meant to live. These skills demand commitment and persistence. In this book, take what you like and leave the rest as you gather the recovery tools that resonate with you. Change your thinking, tap into healing power, and live a life-loving lifestyle.

Anxiety is, in part, a manifestation of physical toxicity and/or nutritional deficiency amidst a heightened body sensitivity that will not be medicated or affirmed away. When your body is truly nourished and able to release noxious substances and debris adequately, the miracle begins—a powerful inner healing force is activated, and your mind and body begin to know a deep peace and joy. Attempting mental control of anxiety with affirmations or physical workouts while you continue to feed your body destructive foodless foods is futile and damaging. Or, conversely, feeding your body with whole plants while being overly critical with yourself will not work. Habitually drinking alcohol while running marathons won't work either. Health anxiety DOES have a bit of truth whispering to you underneath its painful relentlessness and irrationality: there is something truly toxic festering in your body and soul; it's not all in my head needing some kind of psychiatric fix. Much of mental illness does result from toxicity and deficiency that can be helped or healed with a drugless, life-affirming lifestyle. Your body is asking, demanding that you make lifestyle changes in how you relate and care for your body, so health and peace can be yours. Your mind is asking for spiritual and emotional serenity to keep anxiety away at its root. Anxiety management includes caring for the mind, the body, and the spirit. If the body isn't right, the mind isn't right, and the spirit isn't right. All three must be addressed for what hurts one will hurt the other two. Likewise, what helps one will help the other two.

Healing anxiety requires a multifaceted approach of transforming the body, mind, and spirit. The healing methods of this book are divided into four messages: 1) attaining true health thereby decreasing the risk of illness and terror, 2) subverting and managing anxiety while it lurks about and then suddenly strikes, 3) strengthening the communication of the left and right brain as they work together and 4) maintaining balance of body, mind, and spirit. It's time to teach your body, mind, and spirit to sing in harmony as you bask in radiant, fearless health.

Chapter One:
Anxiety Neurophysiology

Though only two percent of body weight, the brain is the highest energy consumer of any organ in the body. Let us fathom the brain to understand how problematic anxiety can be when it manifests within this three-pound organ containing about 86 billion nerve cells (Voytek, 2013). Each neuron is connected to as many as 100,000 other neurons with over 100 chemical messengers formulating an infinite message pathway complex. This pathway complex produces thoughts, feelings, and mental states, including the potential for mystical awareness and consciousness when conditions allow for this illumination. The brain's structures, pathways, and chemicals may produce experiential states from agony to ecstasy. It is our neurotransmitters, known as the agents of awareness, that greatly determine our mental and emotional states. We want and need them in adequate supply for intact mental health.

Although the brain seeks balance, the brain does what it is used to doing as messages flow along established nerve pathways, processing information as slowly as one mph or as fast as 268 mph. Habitual negative thinking is both the cause and the result of repetitive thoughts and emotions traveling certain brain pathways repeatedly, becoming ruts of obsession and rumination. These well-traveled ruts provoke irrational interpretations of various common perceptions: a freckle, an itch, a heart thump, a bloated belly. All these things and more can cause an attack of anxiety. Thankfully, these neuronal pathways are soft-wired rather than hard-wired. They can be rewired to make new connections capable of restoring and maintaining rational thinking, calmness, and peace.

Agents of Awareness: The Neurotransmitters

An overly sensitive fear center, the amygdala, is not the only culprit of an anxiety disorder. It is our own neurotransmitters made in our own bodies that carry messages from one nerve cell to another via electrical impulses that also determine our mental and emotional states. There are one hundred or more neurotransmitters in the brain that are either excitatory or inhibitory of feeling, thought, and function. Animals and even plants use some of the same neurotransmitters as humans, i.e. serotonin and dopamine.

A neurotransmitter is as effective as its receptor, and different brains vary in abundance of receptors. Less receptor availability results in greater vulnerability towards dysphoria and substance abuse to compensate for neurotransmitter deprivation and self-medicate that dysphoria. Psychotropic drugs of abuse such as cocaine, alcohol, and heroin merely manipulate neurotransmitter release or inhibition; this is what creates the high. It is the neurotransmitter stimulation in the brain and *not* the drug that gives the sought after pleasure rush. The drug either squeezes out neurotransmitters like dopamine (pleasure) or gamma amino butyric acid (calming) or blocks reuptake of specific neurotransmitters, so there is more in the space (synapse) between the nerves to keep stimulating the neuron. These fundamental brain messengers are stored and released in the vesicles at the end of each neuron and not present in an infinite supply. That is why drug seeking and addiction is a losing game.

Neurotransmitters depend upon amino acids (protein building blocks that ultimately come from plants) to be manufactured and utilized. Most production of neurotransmitters occurs while you are sleeping. Excessive stress exhausts neurotransmitters and the SAD diet does not serve to replenish them adequately with its fare of processed carbohydrates, animal food, and lack of adequate phytonutrients (Greger 2012). Excessive or inadequate levels of neurotransmitters lead to mania, depression, psychosis, anxiety, and other mental mishaps. Dysphoric emotions and negative thoughts tend to go down the same old negative rut. More people are taking antidepressants today than at any other time in psychiatric history.

Chapter One: Anxiety Neurophysiology

How powerful then are our neurotransmitters! They are the most complex chemicals nature has ever created. They underlie every thought, emotion, and memory as well as many somatic functions as digestion, heartbeat, and blood clotting. Although some brains may struggle with neurotransmitter and/or receptor imbalance, the mind can overcome this limitation with a life-affirming lifestyle of prayer, exercise, a plant-based diet, and thought management.

Let's take a brief look at these messengers. Gamma amino butyric acid (GABA) is an amino acid, and it functions as a widespread inhibitory neurotransmitter, the brain's slow down and stop signal throughout the brain. Inhibition provided by GABA allows the brain to sort through the vast incoming stimuli and use only what is needed to react appropriately, such as when the cortex communicates with other areas in the brain in an orderly manner. The brain's 'go' signal is the excitatory neurotransmitter glutamate of which GABA serves to balance, as every go needs a stop and vice versa in the brain and body. There are GABA receptors all over the brain, with the limbic system having the heaviest concentration. Everyone loves GABA, for it gives such peace and tranquility. Insufficient GABA results in relentless anxiety and panic attacks plus insomnia. This neurotransmitter is depleted by excessive stress, anger, and anxiety that decreases GABA's ability to temper warning messages, allowing these anxiety-ridden messages from the amygdala to bombard and overwhelm the thinking cortex. Alcohol and long-term benzodiazepine use (Valium, Xanax, Ativan, and others) stimulate release of GABA, and after a period of time exhaust its supply leading to a return of anxiety as these drugs become less effective, a process known as tolerance. So forget the drugs, let lifestyle be the GABA provider.

Serotonin is the widespread balancing, calming, and pain modulating neurotransmitter. It is the neurotransmitter with the most wide-ranging impact on the anxiety/peace continuum. Serotonin helps the pre-frontal cortex (PFC) focus and influences self-esteem, appetite, sleep, memory, thermoregulation, and impulse control. When decreased through trauma, illness, pain, prolonged stress, inadequate sleep and nutrient intake, most of the brain has less regulation, and problems are perceived as more intractable and magnified. This further antagonizes an overly sensitized amygdala, leading to increased rumination and obsessive compulsive disorder, sensitivity to threat and doom feelings, depression, anxiety, panic, trembling, insomnia, decreased frustration tolerance, angry outbursts, and impulsiveness. Irritable bowel can flare up. Although both anxiety and depression involve serotonin imbalance, it has been said that anxiety disorders are more difficult to heal than depression (Nedley 2015). Perhaps because the fear response is integral to survival and when augmented by an enlarged and sensitized amygdala, irrational fear responses are more challenging to break.

Surprisingly, ninety-five percent of serotonin is manufactured in the small intestine and five percent in the brain. Serotonin is made from the amino acid tryptophan found in bananas, chocolate, figs, as well as nuts and seeds such as almonds, cashews, walnuts, pumpkin, sesame, and sunflower seeds. Folate (found in greens), magnesium, and vitamin B6 (blueberries, mushrooms, and lentils) are also needed to produce serotonin. Consuming a tryptophan poor diet for even a short time lowers mood and elevates anxiety. Production of serotonin is increased with tryptophan rich food, exercising, being in sunlight, deep sleeps, and stress management. The anti-stress hormone, oxytocin, is released when one feels close to another, including beloved animals. Oxytocin also helps to blunt pain and inflammation, inhibits the amygdala, and increases endorphins and dopamine.

Norepinephrine functions as both a neurotransmitter and a hormone made in the adrenal glands, gastrointestinal lining, and brain. As a neurotransmitter it modulates the brain's reaction to stress and stimulates arousal, helping to regulate mood. As a hormone it initiates the fight-or-flight response, regulates blood pressure, heart rate, and dilates bronchi. Excessive norepinephrine increases tension, nervousness, panic attacks, and magnification of problems. Decreased serotonin and increased norepinephrine brought on with poor sleeping, inadequate nutrition, and frantic stress is a combination that guarantees an anxious mind.

Dopamine regulates physical movement and motivates eating and reproduction, and it helps one seek after rewards such as a job promotion or romance with blissful, secure feelings. Fifty percent of it is made in the gastrointestinal lining. Dopamine reinforces behavior whether healthy or unhealthy, as long as that behavior brings pleasant to ecstatic feelings, since the reward circuit in the brain is hardwired to feel good. These behaviors may be healthy (going for a run that gives surges of wellbeing) or detrimental (inadequate sleep from staying up late or taking drugs to get high). Even thoughts and activities that anticipate a reward will stimulate dopamine release like when you plan a vacation, seek reassurance, or eat foodless foods. So, it makes a lot of sense to choose healthy behaviors and habits as dance, gardening, or meditation and prayer to promote dopamine surges to reinforce behaviors that won't tear you to shreds.

Endorphins (from the words endogenous (inner) and morphine) are bliss-promoting and natural-painkilling neuropeptides that are made in the hypothalamus and released by the pituitary gland during vigorous exercise, emotional stress, pain, romantic interludes, meditation, and deep breathing. Although alcohol, anabolic steroids, and opiates like morphine, heroin, and codeine increase endorphins, so does laughter, music, singing, dance, lavender oil, acupuncture, chocolate, chili peppers, and massage. People with fibromyalgia and obsessive-compulsive disorder have lower baseline levels of endorphins but can increase endorphin levels with daily exercise, laughing, and perchance eating a chili pepper. Many people dread the thought of exercising, but once it becomes a habit, they like the endorphin waves of repose so much that they come to dread the thought of not exercising.

Keeping neurotransmitters balanced is essential for anxiety management. Staying calm amidst strife with calm breathing and relaxed muscles further helps neurotransmitters do their work to sustain an upbeat and productive mood allowing the pre-frontal cortex to stay in charge.

Brain Functions

Understanding some key brain functions gives insight as to what makes irrational anxiety tick.

The pre-frontal cortex (PFC) is found within the largest lobe of the brain—the frontal lobe—located behind the forehead. The PFC is the CEO of the mind, receiving and analyzing all information before making a final decision. The frontal lobe is the control center for all conscious brain functions where will, decision, analysis, morality, and spirituality lies (Nedley 2015). It empowers self-restraint and is closely involved in emotional well-being. Intuition and general intelligence come together here. The frontal lobe is sensitive to harmful lifestyle habits as alcohol and drug use, disorganization, excessive stimulation and clutter, low carbohydrate diet, syncopated, booming music, excessive negative mind states, lack of abstract thinking, acting against one's conscience, addictive behavior, and excessive trance-like screen use. Anxiety decreases frontal lobe circulation, which leads to apathy, impulsiveness, decreased attention, and more anxiety. The PFC of the frontal lobe can become overwhelmed trying to free itself from the overactive and overheated limbic system and is then less able to take control of catastrophic thinking and calm the limbic system (the emotional brain). The PFC needs to be strong enough with adequate neurotransmitters and effective nerve pathways to manage thoughts and emotions, inhibit impulsive and primitive brain reactions (such as not assaulting someone when angry), and to think versus panicking when crisis hits. Too little serotonin in the PFC interferes with shifting away from negativity or seeing a positive perspective. Fortifying the PFC and frontal lobe with a plant based, tryptophan rich diet, meditation, beautiful music, higher math calculations, prayer, exercise, sunlight, yoga, and reasonable thinking restores its rightful role as leader of the brain, making the final appraisal of any threatening information and telling the emotional limbic circuit to relax and move on.

The orbital frontal cortex (OFC) contains working memory and is where brainstorming occurs. These two functions, the PFC and the OFC, help control fear with optimistic, problem-solving activity. Neurotransmitter imbalance leads to the OFC firing more frequently with a sense of danger coming in shoots. Too little serotonin here leads to poor impulse control and irrational reactions to problems.

The anterior cingulated gyrus (ACG) of the cortex is a fold in each hemisphere close to the center of the brain and is known as the vice-president to the CEO. It is responsible for cognitive flexibility and receives details from the hippocampus and emotions from the amygdala and puts them together for analysis. It functions as a filter and amplifier of information and organizes rational calming thoughts to send to the CEO. When the ACG is enlarged and/or does not have a balance of serotonin, it perseverates on negative feelings and is less able to shift rational calming thoughts to the CEO or send analysis back to the amygdala. Serotonin is needed to shift gears in thoughts smoothly, prevent ruminating, and allow the PFC to overrule worry and take charge.

Organ from Hell—Amygdala Gone Wild

Let's go into more detail about the brain's fear center, located in two almond shaped neural clusters known as the amygdalae (singular: amygdala). They are found in the center of the brain resting on top of the brain stem, one in each brain hemisphere. The amygdala is the main appraiser of potentially threatening stimuli. It constantly scans for trouble and warns the brain of danger, with two thirds of its neurons processing negative stimuli while one third of its neurons process positive stimuli. An emotional smoke detector, it registers all emotions as fear, hate, love, anger, and courage, but it has a heightened sensitivity for threatening perceptions potential or real, giving it a bias towards negativity. Negative experiences are stored immediately while positive experiences need to be held in the mind relatively longer in order to be stored in memory.

Anxiety begins in the more primitive and emotionally laden amygdala, yet ultimately, the primary goal of the amygdala is to protect you from harm. This warning function was designed as a survival mechanism to protect one from savagery, fire, predators, and other dangers. Similar to many other animals, we are hard wired for danger detection. In Urbach-Wiethe disease, a rare genetic disorder involving a calcified amygdala, a person experiences no fear in situations that would normally terrify anyone else. Destruction of the amygdala can produce the Kluver-Bucy syndrome which results in fearlessness and disinhibition of behavior. Sociopaths lack fear, conscience, and morality, all functions in which the amygdala plays a part. Life without a fear response would be abnormal and put one at a very high risk for accident and injury. Life would not be as experientially rich either. An anxiety disorder, however, involves an exaggerated fear response that stems from certain brain structures, stress hormones, and mental conditioning that is only destructive to one's mind and body.

As soon as the amygdala perceives threatening stimuli, it sends a message to the hypothalamus that then activates the adrenal glands to secrete epinephrine, the immediate and powerful stress hormone also known as adrenaline used to revive people in cardiac arrest. It travels 250 miles per hour in the body and goes everywhere, causing an increase in heart rate, breathing, blood pressure, sweating, trembling, cold limbs, tight muscles including the throat and chest making it harder to breathe, and increases hydrochloric acid, which promotes gastric ulcers and indigestion. Epinephrine increases blood pressure, and when it is chronically high, it increases atherosclerotic plaque damaging arteries, which hurts the heart, lung, liver, and kidneys. This is a very large reason why anxiety has to be reined in and not run amok.

The amygdala responds with one-trial learning such as learning not to touch a hot pot on the stove. It memorizes a painful, fearful event and its associations immediately. For example, remembering a frightening story of someone dying may activate a fear response if you experience any similar symptoms that that person had. In contrast, the frontal lobe appraises reality in a complex and detailed manner and is constantly testing reality. The amygdala does not reality test and is prone to false alarms. It is responsible for that sharp in-breath when frightened. The amygdala uses foreboding imagination and too many primitive warning signals to create a dramatic response such as, "It's a bear! No, it's a shadow. This headache feels like a brain tumor! I could go into shock from this strange bee sting!"

This will overwhelm the frontal lobe and impede its ability to rationally dismiss catastrophic thinking. Common innocent sensations can intensify when mediated by an overly active amygdala. Anxiety feeds itself when the alarmed amygdala stimulates the adrenals to release more stress hormones, which in turn further stimulates the amygdala. Round and round. At times, very embarrassingly, little will stimulate the amygdala, welling up psychic pain and despair while using up much mental energy.

The amygdala works in close contact with the thalamus, which is the brain switchboard that sends a threatening stimulus immediately to the amygdala for alarm processing. The hypothalamus controls the autonomic nervous system, which regulates fight/flight and rest/digest responses. The hippocampus is the brain's search engine and chief memory processing center. It decides which short-term memories will be stored as long-term memories and connects memories to emotions. These structures are known as the limbic system: the emotional brain that is located under the cortex. The limbic system is tightly connected to the thinking frontal lobe. They are designed to work in harmony with the frontal lobe and make finely tuned decisions such as evaluating how realistic a stressor is and telling the amygdala if its reaction is unwarranted. While an anxiety disorder botches up this design, a new mind and way of living restores this essential chain of command. What can stop this reflexive pattern? The answer lies with the PFC staying in charge of the amygdala and taming stress hormones.

Cortisol: Friend but Potential Foe

The wiring of the amygdala and hypothalamus is so fast that the stress cascade and fear circuit is activated before the thinking brain has a chance to fully process what's happening. After the initial surge of epinephrine subsides, the hypothalamus activates the pituitary gland to send adrenocorticotropic hormone to the adrenal glands to secrete the stress hormone cortisol. Have you ever asked why we don't cascade out of control when stress hits? The answer is cortisol—a life sustaining steroid hormone that is essential in maintaining homeostasis and stress management. It is the main stress hormone and is also involved in regulating blood glucose levels, metabolism of food, anti-inflammation, blood pressure, and central nervous system activation. Cortisol levels vary throughout the day. They are highest in the early morning around 7:00 to 8:00 a.m., then lowest around 3:00 a.m. to 4:00 a.m. Although cortisol is not degraded as quickly as adrenaline is by the kidney and liver, elevated cortisol levels are designed to be short lived. The body and mind needs the right amount of circulating cortisol to be balanced and resilient with clear thinking, immune integrity, thyroid hormone balance, and bone and muscle strength. Intense or unrelenting stress leads to adrenal exhaustion as cortisol is depleted. Exhaustion of mind and body can be intense. Chronically high levels damage insulin receptors, leading to diabetes and cardiovascular disease with increased blood pressure, belly fat, dyslipidemia, and blood sugar dysregulation. Both high and low levels lead to anxiety, depression, insomnia, and obesity.

As stress and cortisol continue to stimulate the amygdala and hippocampus, cortisol receptors are increased in numbers leading to an overly sensitive and enlarged amygdala with less receptors for GABA, the calming neurotransmitter. The amygdala becomes hypervigilant and makes relatively harmless events seem like a threat while it continues to send fear signals to the PFC. The PFC now has trouble suppressing amygdala-generated fear, creating a vicious cycle of stress: anxiety increasing cortisol and cortisol increasing anxiety. Sustained high cortisol is neurotoxic to the hippocampus, making it more difficult to find and make new memories. The hippocampus then has trouble shutting down stress due to difficulty discerning what is safe from unsafe. This leads to feeling unsafe and fearful and not knowing why.

Chronically elevated stress hormones norepinephrine, cortisol, and adrenaline are poisonous to the body and mind much like a motor idling too high for too long heats up and wears out the motor. Thoughts and emotions feel overly urgent with small stressors.

It is very important to relax after stress subsides in order to return cortisol to baseline levels. Soothing activities such as listening to or playing music, journaling, or stretching lessen amygdala hyperreactivity and work to reverse hippocampus damage and strengthen the PFC.

Right Brain and Left Brain

The brain is divided down the middle with two hemispheres, each half working independently and in concert with each other. The left side of the brain encodes learned information, routine, linear structure of perception, math, language, and labeling (including emotions) as well as analysis of detail. It thinks in language and projects the brain chatter we are all familiar with as "do laundry now then walk the dogs" message. The left brain reasons and imparts motivation to be optimistic and take action. It utilizes curiosity and assertion. When strong enough the left brain can mediate the fight-or-flight reaction of the fear circuit: "Stay...I can handle this." In contrast, the right brain waits for an imagined catastrophe to happen, especially in tandem with a pumped up amygdala. The left brain can't connect with the right brain when fear images are too powerful and convincing. For example, it may take having thousands of dollars-worth of diagnostic tests and medical consults that show negative results before the right brain can finally be reassured there is no fatality pending and calm down, let alone the loss of self-collectedness and equanimity.

Yet, the right brain sees the big picture of a situation: it is creative and intuitive, thinking in pictures and learning kinesthetically, concerned with the present moment. This is where the deep inner peace circuitry lies according to Jill Bolte Taylor in her book "My Stroke of Insight: A Brain Scientist's Personal Journey." This Harvard brain scientist had a massive left-brain hemorrhagic stroke incapacitating her language ability, cognitive functioning, walking, reading, writing, and memory. It also wiped out judgment and anxiety. Brain chatter went silent, and her body boundaries faded as she felt enveloped by a blanket of enlightenment and euphoria. Her right brain remained intact, causing her to be conscious only of the present. Inner peace is just a thought away, she writes. Being present in the moment and dancing to music intercepts the tendency of our minds to hook into negative patterns of thought and access our deep inner peace circuitry.

In order to avoid a distorted out of control fear reaction regarding a somatic perception, the left PFC needs the help of the right brain with its intuitive and spiritual awareness to produce an objective conclusion about a questionable somatic sensation/perception. The left PFC needs to recognize that the fear circuit is going off again, and the right brain needs to be grounded in stillness to be heard, even by itself. The coordination of the right brain working with the left PFC has the power to transcend irrational terror and create resilience to stress. An imbalanced right and left brain communication, along with chaos in the anterior cingulated gyrus and amygdala, is a situation where somebody needs to be in control. That somebody is going to be the left PFC. We're talking military sergeant somebody that takes no guff from limbic frenzy. Health anxiety may be understood as a combination of overactive brain structures repeatedly sending false messages of alarm to the frontal cortex. The PFC must take control and unlock the jam (Schwartz 1996). Persistent shifting back to the PFC stating, "This isn't me, it's anxiety," will change the neural pathway even if you have to do it initially a thousand times a day.

Health anxiety may be understood as a combination of overactive brain structures repeatedly sending false messages of alarm to the frontal cortex.

The biochemical abnormalities associated with anxiety can be reversed through forming new brain communication pathways and enhancing brain chemistry. For example, consistently asserting, "My body is powered by my God-given healing drive that launches from each cell," while visualizing your body as vibrant and strong, begins a new brain pathway to avoid identifying with another anxiety attack. Start now! The brain functions best with efficient, harmonious communication between neurotransmitters, brain structures, and brain pathways. This harmony and balance is promoted by giving your brain what it needs: exercise, true nutrition, rest, full breathing, release of congestion, appropriate stimulation, sunlight, stress management, spiritual fitness, love, trustworthy relationships, and solid self-esteem. Let's have serenity and access our intuition, the breath of God, with this type of lifestyle. Intuition is magical and powerful—it's healing.

Chapter Two:
Brain Care

Capturing good health does not need to be a bewildering labyrinth where one encounters a hodgepodge of information amidst health challenges that present themselves. No doubt that we want to feel good. No doubt that many of us think about and try to care for ourselves. We want our bones strong, our muscles flexible, our skin smooth and itch free, our teeth white and able to chew, our hair gleaming, and our stomachs content.

But how much do we actively care for our brains other than seeking alertness, sleeping effectively, and avoiding headaches? I want and need my brain to be clear, calm, and efficient without the anxiety mechanism from being set off in my brain. If the brain does not get what it needs, you'll know about it with irritating states of mind like diminished concentration, depression, anxiety, and lots of headaches. The brain craves balance and does not like to be too hot or too dry, go too fast, or become congested with neurotoxins, saturated fat, waste, or excess glucose (sugar)—but it also begins to die without enough glucose, water, and oxygen, so an appropriate balance is vital. The brain wants to clear out stress hormones such as cortisol and norepinephrine, which in excessive amounts are neurotoxic and inflammatory. And although it can bring pleasure, the brain does not

Chapter Two: Brain Care

like alcohol either, as it is another neurotoxin. If the brain is well cared for, anxiety has less of a foothold within the fear circuit. Be gone, I tell you, be gone.

There are obstacles in keeping good health, however, that may be found both inside and outside of each person. Each person is given a deck of health-determining genes, some protective and some not. "Why?" they cry out when a bad gene triggered by poor lifestyle and toxicity manifests in their body bringing misery and anguish. Rather than examine one's lifestyle, the next thought is to go to the doctor and get fixed. Reflexively following the mainstream's direction of how to be healthy and to solve health problems can disconnect one from a conscious relationship with one's body (all the while serving to increase profits for the medical system). Pills! Invasive tests! Exploratory surgery! Huge doses of radiation from high tech CT scans! When will it end?

In May of 2016, it was found that the third cause of death in the USA is medication side effects and medical error according to an eight-year study by researchers at Johns Hopkins University. The medical system is not failsafe, and no one fully knows which genes they have been given, but we can practice proactive health protection. A willy-nilly lifestyle of chips, booze, steak, and sitting around staring at the tube provides a Russian roulette risk of random sickness striking anyone. Habitually or even impulsively indulging in harmful foods or substances, going through life not caring about one's body, and seeing one's body as merely a vehicle for the ego's ambitions and gratifications will end our lives in a most uncomfortable way. In response to this deck of genes I have been given, let me instead support healthy genes and suppress the unhealthy ones with wisdom and self-care. Then I win this lottery of soaring through life with the greatest of health and happiness.

The problem is that we are conditioned from a young age to make choices that do not support our health, whether we make poor decisions in our diet or by taking drugs or even applying many kinds of lotions and other chemicals that can be harmful. There is powerful conditioning from the food industry that influences our taste sensations and food choices. It begins in infancy and continues relentlessly throughout our life spans. This conditioning is heavily promoted, despite the dominant western diet being (slowly or quickly) deadly. As babies, we are overly vaccinated and come to believe that the physician and medication are the main protectors of our health, but the simple truth is that the majority of disease results from deficiency of nutrients and excessive toxicity of body—something we can control.

When I was a child, the USDA designed nutrition guidelines with big, shiny posters all through elementary school that veiled an agenda to heavily promote daily meat and dairy consumption for robust health. It was a marketing tool to make sure that we children grew up to buy and continue consuming those toxic foods while we unknowingly contributed to the immense suffering that modern agriculture brings. In addition to becoming addicted to Franken-foods as refined sugar and flour, I did not break away from this powerful conditioning for many years. And now the World Health Organization (WHO) in 2015 announced that processed red meat *is* carcinogenic and that all other meats are *probably* carcinogenic. Another misleading recommendation is to drink red wine in (using the politically correct and loop hole term) "moderation." This recommended moderation is a vague measurement while research shows that for women who drink more than one glass of wine a day increase their risk of breast cancer.

Health information is heavily financed by Big Food, Big Wine, Big Salt, and Big Sugar that have political interests influencing what will and will not be promoted for the health of the common human today. Reams of dietary information create confusion that serves to keep people mindlessly consuming that which hurts them. This confusion acts as a clever strategy as people throw up their hands and just eat what they want and enjoy.

"No one knows what's best!" People say, "I am going to enjoy my life! Please pass the chops." And the destructive chops continue to be purchased, cooked, and eaten. Many baby boomers now live to see the horror of their loved ones dying miserably and unnecessarily of diseases that could have been prevented. We boomers have come to rebel from this fate. Thanks to the Internet, the truth of healthy eating may be revealed, albeit with much critical thinking, at the touch of a finger providing life-saving guidance on what to eat. Let's sum it up right now with Michael Pollan's (2009) direction to "Eat food. Mostly plants. Not too much."

Why not practice a protective and health loving lifestyle then? After one gives up rich and carcinogenic food then finding in due time that the craving for these foods has gone, one finds a new appreciation for nutritionally packed food and comes to experience a joy and peace that no chicken nugget or diet soda can replace. Will there be some withdrawal from these pernicious and nocent foods? Well, possibly, but remembering these foodless foods starve our cells and damage tissue leading to cancerous growth and heart disease will help to catapult you through any withdrawal. This lifestyle provides a shield of protection even if you have a sketchy deck of genes.

Chapter Two: Brain Care

A rare few can heavily smoke and drink and "get away with it," living a long but lesser quality of life, having strong genes from birth. They appear fearless and place the pleasure of toxins above anything with the cavalier attitude "live for today for tomorrow you die." The risk of tomorrow bringing a slow suffocation or horrific suffering for months before dying is disregarded or minimized. "No! I will die sweetly in my sleep! No! I will collapse painlessly after my speech!" Let them look around to see the obesity, the grim faces, the struggle to run or dance. "No, I gotta have a few belts of beer before I get out on that dance floor." How many people over the age of forty are free from medications or chronic diseases? This denial and minimization of God-forsaken consequences is the common human way. It is essential to remember that a living ninety-five-year old who smoked and drank most of his or her life is a rare exception and that most who follow this destructive lifestyle die prematurely or suffer chronic pain and dysfunction before they die.

It is true that many of our grandparents did not live in a sea of pesticides and heavy metals; they were more likely to eat from their own gardens and work hard. Still, it is highly likely that that ninety-five-year old is hobbling around with some sort of chronic disability and wishing he or she were free of that ache and pain. It is notable that the elderly practicing a largely plant-based, very active lifestyle are largely free of such disabilities.

If you don't take care of your body, then your risk of developing illness and terror rises exponentially.

The truth is if you don't take care of your body, then your risk of developing illness and terror rises exponentially. This relentless anxiety disorder is progressive. I suggest getting in gear and staying in gear—none of this back and forth nonsense either. You will simply pay. The easier, softer way will not work. Recovery comes with dedication and gut wrenching hard work. Have a problem with this? Mercilessly, suck it up or go back to a Russian roulette life where each day can become a crapshoot.

Near Infinite Expressions of the Body

We know by now that the body is not some inert thing pumping blood and loving food. Let's list some health challenges that can cause anxiety:

hyperthyroid (thyroid gone berserk), Addison's disease, Cushing's disease, adrenal exhaustion and pheochromocytoma (adrenals out of whack), partial and generalized seizures, labyrinthitis (inner ear inflammation), head injuries, asthma, hypertension, mitral valve prolapse (bulging heart valve) and other heart dysfunctions, drug use and withdrawal, fibromyalgia, allergies and food intolerances, glucose intolerance, heavy metal accumulation, decreased estrogen/hormone imbalances, hiatal hernia and esophageal spasms, chronic obstructive pulmonary disease, and decreased levels of magnesium, vitamin B's, vitamin D, and calcium. Just about any dysfunction or deficiency can lead to feeling anxious.

The automatic part of our nervous system is known as the autonomic nervous system (ANS). It takes care of things beyond our conscious control such as our heartbeat and digestion. It has two branches: the sympathetic (arouse and heat up) and the parasympathetic (release and cool down) nervous systems. The sympathetic nervous system, which manifests the fight-or-flight reaction, can become a pesky, all too often besetment. Anxiety (even unknown stimuli) leads to this fight-or-flight state, and the body responds with increased blood pressure, heart rate, and respiratory rate. The fight-or-flight response may also cause dizziness, blurred vision, clumsiness, unclear thinking, derealization (reality feels dreamlike), muscular tension and spasms, sweating profusely, heart palpitations, abdominal discomfort and diarrhea, shortness of breath, increased urination, trembling, numbness, dryness of mouth and throat, lump feeling in throat, choking, coughing, headaches, tingling, itching, twitching, tinnitus (ringing in ears), rectal pain, rashes, and unexplained vomiting.

Any of these manifestations can provoke catastrophic interpretation and a perpetual sense of ill health. Yet, everyone experiences some changes with excretion, abdominal cramping, and/or nausea at times. The body has a big job to do running itself as though it is a big ship. It goes through changes sometimes for no apparent reason throughout every day, week, month, year, and decade. This can all be very normal. No one's body is 100 percent symmetrical. There are an infinite number of symptoms and combinations of sensations we can experience in our lifetimes. Sensations wax and wane randomly. They are very real, frequent, and tangible. But they are benign. Focusing on these sensations magnifies them while distractions diminish them. We can learn to see these sensations as just sensations versus every sensation as an impending disaster.

The parasympathetic nervous system (PSNS) brings peace back into the body and mind. This calming system decreases the stress hormone cortisol, heart rate, and blood pressure, while simultaneously increasing

Chapter Two: Brain Care

blood flow to the brain, augmenting immunity, and decreasing pain, anxiety, and depression. We can live without a sympathetic nervous system flying or fighting although at a greater safety risk, but we cannot survive without a parasympathetic nervous system to rest and digest. Deep breaths, stretching muscles, and releasing tears instead of holding back sadness can help resume the PSNS in calming the body and mind. Vulnerability is seen as loss of control and is not the sympathetic nervous system's bag, yet holding back tears and emotions can give you a lingering lump in your throat known as *globus hystericus*, which is many little throat muscles that remain contracted due to unrelenting stress.

Because the self-healing response is dependent upon the PSNS to work while relaxed, the fight-or-flight response of an anxiety attack secretes stress hormones that impair self-healing mechanisms. Healing energy is diverted into the emergency mode and health maintenance becomes a lower priority (Rankin 2013). When the sympathetic nervous system (SNS) is highly activated in the fight-or-flight mode, non-essential systems shut down as in the gastrointestinal and immune systems. This means rogue cell disposal is hampered and slowed down. Very little body healing will occur then (Rankin 2013).

Being aware of one's body (and feeling empathy for another) lights up the insula located near the anterior cingulated gyrus. We now know that the awareness our insula provides can be usurped by out of control imagination, as we confuse random stimulation of the autonomic nervous system (sweating, shaking, feeling hot) with true distress signals. At times, random anxiety, in addition to nervous system blips, mean nothing other than this strange little body that you were given is simply being alive.

Remind yourself that you have been here before, survived it, and will survive again.

Many people accept having sensations without ever having a clear medical explanation for them. I woke one day to a swollen and irritated right side of my throat lasting two days, then my left rib ached with shooting pain, and then heartburn and fullness from the hiatal hernia sliding around. Bafflingly, health anxiety makes you forget that the current sensation has happened many times in the past. Remind yourself that you have been here before, survived it, and will survive again. Drawing on past experiences provides a knowledge baseline of our expressive bodies, and we can quickly say, "I know this feeling; it's nothing." Instead of expecting sensations to go away for good, practice accepting somatic yips and dips that happen in a somewhat unpredictable manner. Challenge yourself every day: "I don't care if I am having x, y, or z sensation again. This sensation is an opportunity to stand up to it and pull its cover of fear and uncertainty."

The Mind Bone is Connected to the Body Bone

Here is a partial list of somatic manifestations that the body may express when stressed, congested or seemingly for no reason at all:

Head:
migraines; light-headedness; insomnia; brain fog; sinus congestion. Migraines involve dilation of scalp arteries causing pressure on nerves. These scalp arteries are very sensitive to stress and irritants (like histamine and tyrosine in red wine and aged cheeses), and when they reach a certain point of buildup, a migraine ensues. No! A migraine may be relieved without drugs by releasing colon contents as well as applying warmth below the head and cold on the head, ...which dilates the peripheral vessels and constricts the cranial ones to shunt blood away from the scalp.

Eye:
dryness to the point that one eye is or both eyes are blurry; spastic eye, where vision becomes a whirling blender for a few seconds; spatial disorientation, which is when one sees stripes or tiny squares; itchy, heavy, and/or sore eyes.

Mouth:
burning and/or dry mouth; canker sores; metallic tastes; blisters; geographic tongue (map like tongue); burning and/or blistered lips.

Throat and trachea:
globus hystericus (knot or lump feeling in throat due to stress); mouth and throat blood blisters that rupture (Angina Bullosa Hemorrhagica); slowed and chaotic swallowing; broncho- and esophageal spasm; dryness; swelling; congestion; tonsiliths, otherwise known as tonsil stones, which cause inflammation and another opportunity for fear to strike: "What the heck are those strange little things?"

Ears:
labyrinthitis; Meniere's disease; vestibular disorders; tinnitus; wax impaction; diminished hearing. The inner ear and mental equilibrium are deeply connected. When the inner ear is infected, inflamed,

or congested, it causes vertigo and a dissociated feeling from reality along with severe dysphoria and feeling out of control. This can last for weeks to months as the acoustic nerve heals millimeter by millimeter. The delicate labyrinth of the inner ear is filled with tiny specialized hairs and otoliths (tiny grains) fed by microcirculation. A high fat and/or salt diet can congest this microcirculation resulting in vestibular dysfunction. One may find significant relief by avoiding ANY added salt that will prevent and reduce edema in the labyrinth. However, added salt is ubiquitous: restaurants, packaged and prepared foods, meals created by well-meaning loved ones may all contain added salt. Although the inner ear is the dominating organ for giving balance, the brain is also dependent on joint, tendon, and skeletal muscle positioning and movement to register balance and feel grounded. Therefore, walking or even bouncing the foot compensates for the terrible floating feeling. As lingering labyrinthitis can be agonizing, Klonopin (a benzodiazepine) gives mercy and is a humane remedy to counteract the spatial disorientation and imbalanced floating feeling while the ear struggles to regain equilibrium.

Gut:
irritable bowel syndrome; bloating and cramping; nausea and vomiting; constipation; diarrhea; hiatal hernia; esophageal spasms; gas pains; heartburn from gastro-esophageal reflux disease (GERD), which can cause heart dysrythmias; hemorrhoids; anal fissures. Less than one stool released each day (done without struggling) promotes reabsorption of poisons, hemorrhoids, diverticulosis, anal fissures, rectal spasms, and migraine headaches. Magazines and books kept by the toilet is the mark of a constipated home. Prevent constipation with fruits, vegetables, and legumes high in fiber along with adequate water and exercise. Apples and ground flax seeds with adequate water intake are especially effective for regular, easy to pass stools.

Heart and chest:
dysrhythmias (heart beating erratically but without chest pain, dizziness, or difficulty breathing usually means nothing); atrial fibrillation (upper chamber of heart quivering instead of pumping blood down to lower ventricles); vaso-vagal reactions (vagus nerve suddenly slows heart rate down leading to near fainting or fainting); chest wall pain; fluctuating blood pressure; increased respiratory rate, which is so common with anxiety and panic attacks. Breathing faster increases alkalinity too quickly, disrupting the nervous system with tingling fingers, light-headedness, and more anxiety. Breathing into a paper bag

decreases alkalinity, slows down hyperventilating, and decreases anxiety.

Endocrine:

adrenal exhaustion; hypothyroid; blood glucose fluctuations.

Skin:

rashes; itching; hot and cold sweats; easy bruising; strange eruptions; mucous membrane irritation and inflammation; dry skin; neurodermatitis; cold urticaria (hives when exposed to cold weather).

Pelvic:

diverticulosis; over active bladder; interstitial cystitis; bladder spasms; vulvodynia (pain of vulva); functional proteinuria (bubbly urine); levator ani syndrome, which is an excruciatingly painful benign lower pelvic neuro-muscular disorder that causes lower pelvic and rectal spasms. Place heat to area for relief and know it will end in a few minutes.

Muscle, joint, and myofascial-pain, spasms, pinched nerves:

A plant-based diet is high in magnesium, the calming mineral for 640 muscles, along with millions of tiny muscles controlling the hairs in skin and in the smooth muscles of the intestines, internal organs, and blood vessels. I believe fibromyalgia, a syndrome characterized by fatigue and chronic pain in muscles and tissues, results when an accumulation of toxins and irritants such as heavy metals, pathogens, histamine, stress, and metabolic byproducts irritate nerves and tissues. Such irritants may also include unpleasant smells, synthetic fabric on skin, and negative and sensationalistic media along with daily uncertainties that can be intolerable. "What now? Why?" Coping with this syndrome requires an anti-inflammatory diet, hydration, exercise, and deep tissue massage.

Histamine intolerance may be part of this somatic hyperreactivity. Those with health anxiety and a reactive body may have a greater histamine release in response to various stressors. Histamine is a nitrogenous compound that is released by mast cells (a type of white blood cell) in reaction to injury, stress, or allergy and initiates inflammation. Histamine also functions to regulate many physiologic functions as in stimulating the stomach to secrete hydrochloric acid, sleep-wakefulness regulation, and vasodilatation. During seasonal allergy times, histamine goes wild. Highest concentrations of histamine are found in the skin, stomach, and lung. Release of histamine, which can be very irritating to tissues, can lead to itching, swelling, hives, running nose, muscle spasm, bronchoconstriction, throat tightening, and loss of voice. Excessive histamine levels can also evoke indigestion, migraines, heart dysrhythmias, insomnia, dizziness, body temperature dysregulation, abdominal pain, anxiety, panic, confusion, and fatigue.

Foods that either have a high histamine content or provoke histamine release in the body include vinegar, fermented foods, aged foods, processed meat, alcoholic drinks, strawberries, avocados, spinach, citrus fruit, tomatoes, dried fruit, mushrooms, soy, walnuts, and cashews. Consuming a low histamine diet for a few weeks and then slowly adding histamine inducing foods back can reveal one's tolerance and help prevent symptoms, namely anxiety, from reemerging. Specific food is not the only histamine raising element, unfriendly intestinal flora and stress such as cold weather and emotional upheaval do as well. Dehydration also raises histamine levels.

During seasonal allergy time, one would need to double efforts to keep histamine levels from spilling over into outward symptoms. Combat histamine intolerance by minimizing high histamine foods, dressing very warmly, breathing deeply, and meditating in order to soothe dysphoric states (unpleasant feelings). It is important to control the amount of inflammation in one's body that leads to excessive histamine release from mast cells. Natural anti-histamines include oil of oregano, green juice, thyme, coriander, sweet potato, holy basil, stinging nettle, elderberry, ginkgo, fennel, garlic, chamomile, green tea, carrots, leafy greens, oil of evening primrose, ginger, cardamom, and parsley.

The brain-immune-endocrine system, or mind-body connection, can lead to many unexplained symptoms along with a lower pain threshold, but they are very real. Many of these somatic manifestations cannot be diagnostically measured, as they may involve minute biochemical abnormalities related to subtle chemical and/or electrical imbalances that are not detected by diagnostics. Sensations and signs can be bizarre and baffle a medical doctor, who may process the complaint with diagnostic procedures and specialists; this just escalates anxiety while you wait for the results only to be told the sensation appears to be of a psychiatric nature. Psychiatry tends to drug away these complaints, and there is little healing there. Learning some basics about your body empowers you to be in charge of understanding and coping with these erratic manifestations.

One Notch Further: The Highly Sensitive Mind and Body

Each body has a continuum of sensitivity and reactivity. Some people can have lifestyles of chips, shots of whiskey, and erratic sleeps and still appear to fly through this rough living (for awhile). They enjoy movies depicting terror, can work long hours, and give dinner parties for fifteen people without feeling overwhelmed or exhausted. Others need frequent solitude, have reactions to certain foods, and feel happiest hiking in the mountains or discussing art, poetry, or philosophy. In her book, *The Highly Sensitive Person*, Elaine N. Aron, PhD, describes the highly sensitive nervous system and how to live with this ultimate blessing.

A person who is highly sensitive may have:

1. Heightened anxiety beginning at a young age.
2. Feelings of being overwhelmed with excessive stimuli and more awareness of discomforts, sensations, and manifestations, such as increased sensation to cold, hunger, illness, drugs, sounds, fabric, crowds, lights, startle reflex and fatigue.
3. Strong rich emotions and a sense of injustice.
4. Intensity/difficulty with relationships. They may feel alienated, shy, or easily hurt.
5. Sensitivity to suffering and death.
6. Vivid dreams in color that are easily remembered.

It is very common for those who are somatic to have a more delicate and reactive nervous system. The body itself can be a source of over arousal, needing peaceful interludes to calm the over aroused state. Self-care becomes essential to manage feeling overwhelmed, chaotic, and anxious. Taking quiet time and seeking solitude offers solace and regeneration from living in a loud and overwhelming world. Eating true food, working the body and mind, and practicing other health supportive activities supports and protects the highly sensitive nervous system. This congruent way of life helps to intercept anxiety attacks that are more prevalent with poor health habits and resulting health problems.

Chapter Two: Brain Care

> *Being highly sensitive is not to be underestimated, for unless you take care of yourself appropriately, you are going to hear about it.*

Being highly sensitive is not to be underestimated, for unless you take care of yourself appropriately, you are going to hear about it. Once during a miserable beach trip with unfriendly peers, I suddenly felt a wave of extreme nausea with sudden sweating, trembling, and heat come over me. I quickly ditched the peers and dashed into a restroom where I laid my cheek down on the cold tile floor desperately trying to get relief despite the less than hygienic conditions. Within a few minutes, the agony dissipated as mysteriously as it had come on. "What was that terrible attack?" I asked. Years later I understood that it was stress mediated serotonin instability and/or histamine buildup coming over me like a wave and then mysteriously fading away. Gain such an understanding of your sensitive mind-body to the point that it is driven into your clearest conviction, so when pain and fear strike, you can remind yourself "Yes, I have this, and I will take solitude, drink a green smoothie, or just move away from this obnoxious person," which serves to intercept a full fear onslaught.

> *Gain such an understanding of your sensitive mind-body to the point that it is driven into your clearest conviction.*

Let's Get Clear About What Isn't Good

Alcohol—what about it? Even though alcohol, especially wine, is wrapped up in glamour and sophistication, it is a depressant drug and cell poison, irritating all tissues that it touches while increasing blood pressure and heart rate in an attempt to get the alcohol out of the body quickly. Alcohol is mostly metabolized in the liver into acetaldehyde, which is thirty times more toxic than alcohol and a known carcinogen. It is a potent poison causing hangovers, headaches, depressed immune system, and liver damage (Trowbridge and Walker 1986). Acetaldehyde is one reason why many people who drink don't go on to become alcoholic as it is responsible for dry heaves that can go on for two days: "Never again!"

The pleasurable feelings that one seeks from alcohol come from an initial increase in dopamine, norepinephrine, endorphins, and GABA. Yet, even when feeling the first flush of inebriation after a few sips, it is already agitating nerves in the brain beginning in the frontal lobes and moving its way across the brain as one keeps drinking. The liver metabolizes about an ounce of alcohol an hour, slightly less than the amount in one drink, a sure-fire way to get a little tipsy. Drinkers manifest cognitive narrowing with less mental flexibility, resulting in emotions being more labile, as for example, impulsive barking at another like "you heard what I said!"

To drink routinely is to choose to have a mild or not so mild lobotomy as one loses finely tuned social graces, precision of thinking, and creativity. Alcohol lowers blood flow to the brain; it is dehydrating and eats up vitamin B's (the nerve vitamins), leaving nerves raw and malnourished. Alcohol can cause depression and anxiety even several days after the last drink due to nerve agitation, increased cortisol, and decreased serotonin and GABA (both essential for anxiety and depression prevention and management). Dopamine levels drop resulting in less pleasure and motivation. Norepinephrine falls affecting memory and the ability to think clearly. Endorphins decrease making one more sensitive to pain and discomfort.

Trying to manage anxiety if one is sleep deprived is like trying to play the piano when you're drunk. Alcohol is not a friend to sleep even though images of downing a shot of vodka and collapsing on the couch seem to portray otherwise. Why? Alcohol depresses and interrupts rapid eye movement (REM) dream state, and deep sleep that is essential for life and coping with anxiety. You may fall asleep, but you're not staying there. Lack of dreaming and deep sleep stimulates the release of the stress hormone cortisol, which promotes insomnia. Cortisol further depresses the immune system—the master healing agent—which will never be fully recharged if exposed to habitual drinking.

None of us like the idea of cancer, especially we health anxietians. I can't stand the word. But let's all clearly know that alcohol is carcinogenic. Alcohol increases your chances of getting sunburn and skin cancer due to oxidative stress, which uses up antioxidants as carotenoids present in the skin and, therefore, provides less protection. Within just eight minutes after a shot of beer, wine, or liquor, the level of carotenoids in the skin decreases dramatically (Greger 2016). Alcohol increases the risk of cancer anywhere in the body, especially the mouth, larynx, esophagus, breast, stomach, colon, liver, and uterus. Who would want to take such a chance? Many do, I know.

For most people, as alcohol wears off, it leaves one dysphoric and secretly looking forward to the next drink to recapture a sense of ease, confidence, and euphoria. For nearly everyone else, alcohol suppresses anxiety making one feel fearless, but it then works against sober anxiety management. For those who are highly sensitive and working to manage anxiety, alcohol can ironically act to disinhibit anxiety: "Wait, I'm not relaxed! I feel worse!" I did have a few rare times when a small amount of wine took a nervous edge off of a fearful musing and showed the falseness of the rumination, a lovely but fleeting moment. But there were more times when half of a glass of wine disinhibited anxiety, and I felt even more nervous. "Forget this," I decided. My stomach could also not stand alcohol and would send immediate demands to my brainstem to just eject this terrible brew right back up the gullet. What a mess.

Ultimately, drinking is just taking a drug to try to escape anxiety. This chemical pursuit weakens one's inner strength, increases the risk of dependency, and irritates the liver, overloading it with fat. We already have sensitive tissues and minds, so why irritate them further with this irritating drug? Why make anxiety worse by drinking alcohol? I recommend small amounts of alcohol very rarely, but secretly, I encourage none at all. Get resveratrol, a potent antioxidant that is found in red wine (conferring an alleged health benefit of red wine) instead from red grapes, peanuts, and blueberries. Your heart and brain will thank you for consuming these beautiful plants instead of alcohol—a drug that your very important organs do not like.

Let's look at a few more substances and behavior that can be unintentionally harmful:

Caffeine:
a stimulant found in coffee, tea, chocolate, energy drinks, some medications, and many carbonated drinks. Caffeine stimulates the adrenal glands to release cortisol, which adds to the adrenal workload and increases heart rate and blood pressure. Caffeine can exacerbate anxiety and panic, and it further interferes with the neurotransmitter adenosine, which brings calm and prepares the body for sleep in the evening. It interferes with the metabolism of some B vitamins such as thiamin (B1), which is needed for the synthesis of GABA (we can't

afford to be short on peaceful, sleep-promoting GABA). We want good sleep and a calm, alert mind. Many self-medicate with caffeine to compensate for the inertia and fatigue that anxiety brings, only to eventually crash into fatigue, insomnia, and more anxiety. Although it takes six hours for half of the amount of caffeine consumed to be eliminated, you may be caffeine sensitive and metabolize it more slowly than others with one cup in the morning, causing you to stare up at the ceiling instead of falling asleep sixteen hours later. Yet, some people can fall asleep right after drinking a cup of coffee. What?? Adrenal exhaustion, maybe? We all have a different tolerance for this drug. If you consume more than 250 mg caffeine (equivalent of 2–3 cups of coffee) per day, you may experience nervousness, muscle twitching, diarrhea, stomach pain, tinnitus, and trembling. On the other hand, caffeine stimulates dopamine and norepinephrine and is liver protective (Greger 2015). So it's one more *ad infinitum* suggestion that if you are going to drink this drug caffeine, please do so with consciousness and care using the following options: none, small amounts infrequently, and not more than one to two cups daily.

Medication:

All drugs are hammers (think of LSD having its profound effect with microgram amounts) and are liver toxic. Most drugs only target specific functions and treat signs and symptoms rather than the root cause of the problem. All have side effects whether or not you feel the effects. Though they have their place in emergencies, we are deeply conditioned to run to them for any malady. The liver is not happy with this arrangement.

Antidepressants:

largely block re-uptake of the monoamine neurotransmitters (serotonin, norepinephrine, or dopamine) of which the brain responds by down regulating neurotransmitter receptors; this is why they lose effect over a period of time. A person may climb onto the antidepressant merry-go-round and try this one then that one or taking more than one, which happens to decrease the seizure threshold. A person may have a first time seizure and then has to be worked up for a brain tumor. Two terrifying shots in one. Antidepressants can affect the rhythm of the heart, increasing the risk for dangerous aberrant rhythms. This neurotransmitter tweaking frequently increases impulsivity and an 'I don't care' attitude. Truly, it is why some people end up killing themselves or others. Though antidepressants have an antihistamine effect, which can decrease levels of anxiety, antidepressants may help only two out of ten with anxiety and/or depression and may cause weight gain, suicidal and compulsive behavior, as well as sleep and sexual problems.

Psychiatric drugs:
affect metabolic pathways and neurochemistry that can change thinking with long-term use. They can diminish frontal lobe integrity and spiritual awareness that helps you to transcend anxiety and depression. They may help with ruminative anxiety initially, but it is often at the cost of a homogenizing effect on the mind as the highs and lows of full and passionate living are flattened out. Joy as well as pain is blunted, and people keep taking them despite not feeling the wellbeing they had desired.

Is there not a better way? Happily, yes. There are natural monoamine oxidase inhibitors such as different kinds of berries, apples, onion, grapes, kale, and green tea (Greger 2013). Just saturate your brain with these lovely polyphenol-infested plants instead of the SAD and see how much better you feel without having a flatter life.

Benzodiazepines, such as Valium, Xanax and Ativan, function as anxiolytics (a drug that relieves anxiety) by increasing the neurotransmitter GABA that then depresses the central nervous system and *voila*! The nervous shoots of tension and worry simmer right down. Sound too good to be true? Well, it is, and addiction is right on the tail of this immediate feel good switch. Benzodiazepines dull cognitive sharpness over time, slowing the mind and body down. Side effects of benzodiazepines alone include: dizziness, headache, confusion, impaired coordination, memory impairment, depression, paresthesias (weird little nerve numbness and/or tingling), syncope (fainting), nightmares, palpitations (irregular or loud heartbeats), chest pain, hypotension (low blood pressure), sore throat/chest congestion, allergic rhinitis (running, inflamed nose), blurred and/or double vision, diarrhea/constipation, nausea/vomiting, abdominal pain, sexual dysfunction, difficulty urinating, muscle cramping, joint pain, dyspnea (labored breathing), increased sweating, dermatitis (skin inflammation), anxiety disinhibition between and during doses, white blood cell (immune cells) decrease, slurred speech, tremor, amnesia, hallucinations, cardio-vascular collapse, nystagmus (horizontally shifting eyes), and liver dysfunction.

What is our usual response to these possible side effects? We either don't think about them or blow them off with: "Won't happen to me." We can become so conditioned to run to drugs that we look the other way regarding these risks and dangers. Along with most drugs, sedating medications such as benzodiazepines are recommended only for emergency needs such as panic states, hyperventilating, no sleep for two days, a psychotic break, or halting seizure activity. They then humanely provide mercy and can be life-saving. Although the severity of psychotic illness requires the use of long-term, anti-psychotic medications in many cases, even psychotic illnesses such as schizophrenia can improve with lifestyle changes and brain reconditioning. Making these changes could mean needing smaller amounts of anti-psychotics required to keep one in remission. Although side effects still occur, these drugs work as a brace for someone who has lost his or her legs either permanently or temporarily.

If you are looking towards forced chemical brain adjustment to solve anxiety, you may find temporary relief, but you will not find the ultimate long-term remedy found in a nourished brain, transformed mind, and vitalized spirit. Routine use of medication cannot fix a malnourished, anxious brain. If I keep taking pills and don't nourish my brain, how effective is that? I have a starved brain on drugs. Let's feed our brain with what it needs: plants and more plants—greens, seeds, and fruit. Let's meditate. Let's dance. Let's do cognitive coaching and heal our thoughts. Whole foods are greatly medicinal and eliminate the need for drugs in a vast number of cases. One's highest thinking and feelings are always diminished with the chronic use of psychotropic drugs. Your body and mind are able to heal while drugs only suppress toxicity and symptoms, requiring the body to turn its energy to metabolizing and excreting the drug versus healing needs. Drugs are synthesized from humanity's hand versus whole plants being created by the true Healer. Which would you guess has the true healing power?

Let's look at how body pH levels come into play. The brain does not like being in an acidic state. There is a fundamental role of brain pH in fear (Maddock 2010). The power of hydrogen, or pH, is the measurement of hydrogen ion concentration ranging from one to fourteen with seven as neutral. A pH lower than seven is acidic and above seven is basic or alkaline. The pH of the brain and body is carefully regulated to keep the acid to alkaline/base level between 7.35 and 7.45 with anything much further from this range being incompatible with life. Some synapses between brain neurons (including the amygdala) have specialized proteins that sense acidity and stimulate neurons when increased acid is detected. A more acidic state heightens anxiety, headaches, confusion, dysrhythmias and increased heart rate, nausea, vomiting, diarrhea, shortness of breath, coughing, abdominal pain, twitching, and lethargy.

Chapter Two: Brain Care 45

The body tends toward metabolic acidosis through normal functions such as respiration, metabolism, and activity. Digested food leaves either an acid or alkaline ash residue. An acidic diet is one filled with meats, fried and fatty foods, dairy, processed and refined sugar, alcohol, carbonated drinks, chocolate, vinegar, artificial sweeteners, smoking, and coffee. This promotes anxiety as the pH of the blood leans toward the acidic range. Processed sugar and alcohol also shoot insulin up that then decreases glucose levels, leading to mood swings and anxiety. It's just a double-edged sword. Dehydration, drugs, and dysphoric emotions increase cortisol and adrenaline that then increase acid levels.

Lactic acid is a breakdown product of glucose metabolism that is constantly being produced and consumed during brain activity. Those with panic disorder tend to generate excess lactic acid in their brains during ordinary mental activities, especially in the acid sensitive fear circuits. Lactic acid is further increased by medications such as metformin and salicylates, excessive exercise, low oxygen levels, alcohol, liver disease, and vitamin B1 (thiamine) deficiency.

Carbon dioxide acts like an acid in the body. People with panic disorder are unusually sensitive to carbon dioxide buildup that increases brain acidity as when holding one's breath or taking shallow breaths. Being near volcanic gases or highly polluted areas, dehydration, vomiting, seizures, sleep apnea, drug overdose, and lung disease can also increase brain acidity. Obesity makes breathing more difficult, and sedative drugs, including alcohol, can interfere with adequate ventilation of the lungs, which causes more carbon dioxide retention.

One of the many beneficial effects of non-extreme aerobic exercise is that metabolically active tissues, including the brain, become more efficient at consuming and removing lactic acid with powerful anti-anxiety effects. Magnesium also decreases lactic acid (found in greens, beans, grains, avocado, bananas, dark chocolate, pumpkin and sesame seeds, almonds, cashews, and peanuts). Hydration helps to clear lactic acid. Try as an experiment: the next time you feel anxious or tense, drink some green juice or smoothie and do some energetic moving about. Then notice where your tension level goes. Who needs a pill?

An alkaline forming plant diet decreases the strain on the body's acid-detoxification systems. Most plants are alkalinizing, although grains (except millet), nuts (except almonds and chestnuts), beans, plums, and cranberries are slightly acidic and can be easily balanced with greens and fruit to prevent higher acidic loads. Once after eating around 15 plums, I felt a wave of nervousness leer up. So now if I eat plums, I mix them with other fruits. An alkaline dominating diet helps maintain a non-anxiety promoting pH level in the body and brain for calmness and restful sleeping.

Arachidonic acid is a pro-inflammatory omega-6 fatty acid that is highest in chicken and eggs and significant in meat and fish. It affects mental health negatively by inflaming the brain. The high amount of uric acid, resulting from animal protein metabolism, also promotes anxiety as well as gout (excruciating large toe pain), heart and kidney disease, and strokes. According to Michael Greger, MD of NutritionFacts.org, inflammation also comes from endotoxins in animal foods, which have very high bacterial loads. An endotoxin is a toxin present inside a bacterial cell that is released when the bacteria disintegrates. Even when animal food is cooked or goes through the acid bath in the stomach, endotoxins remain and are transported into the bloodstream by saturated fat causing inflammation, insulin resistance, atherosclerosis (arterial fat buildup), and arteriosclerosis (stiffened arteries).

Brain inflammation and mental illness are connected according to a report in BioMed Central, 2013. Regular consumption of refined sugar, flour, and fats (that elevate blood sugar and insulin levels) as well as red and processed meats, smoking, and alcohol can increase brain inflammation and provoke anxiety. Other elements that increase brain inflammation and anxiety include sleep deprivation, chronic stress, a sedentary life, and decreased levels of vitamin D. I would further add that added salt, chemicals (for example: nicotine, aspartame, and MSG), dehydration, allergies, and overeating are also irritating to the brain, which if irritated enough can lead to a migraine headache.

American culture puts a large value on consuming animal muscles, fat, and milk. For some this will also include brains, tongues, intestines, livers, hearts, and thyroid glands. The problem is that animal tissue and breast milk have high levels of protein and fat that promotes kidney damage, cancer, and autoimmune diseases. Decomposing cadaver foods create acidic wastes. Consuming animal proteins in amounts greater than five percent of the diet increases tumor development while plant protein decreases tumor development. This is due to enzyme activity that either detoxifies or activates carcinogens depending on amounts of animal protein consumed. Nutrition is far more important in controlling cancer promotion than the dose of the initiating carcinogen (Campbell 2006).

The body struggles to metabolize and excrete this nitrogenous, putrefying waste. The pancreatic digestive enzymes trypsin and chymotrypsin metabolize animal protein. These enzymes also dissolve the protective protein coating around cancerous, rogue cells. Animal protein requires a substantial amount of these enzymes to digest it, but there is a limited supply of these enzymes in the body. Digesting the large amount of animal protein in the SAD takes away from their availability to dissolve the protein coating of a rogue cell. This protective coating makes a rogue cell unrecognizable to the immune system, so it is left alone instead of eliminated. It then multiplies like angry rabbits. These pancreatic enzymes are not required to digest plant protein, so with a plant-based diet, these enzymes remain in plentiful supply to attack and control those pesky rogues of which all of us have at all times in our bodies. And here's the smashing truth—it is our immune system that keeps them from growing into a threatening knot, a knot that can choke the life out of us (Anderson 2009). Glory be to God for this system. So, the concluding point is to eat plants to avoid this and a whole lot of future terror. Rule in recovery: eat well or-- well, it just isn't good.

Eating animals terrorized before death with their flesh full of massive stress hormones does not sound like an appropriate diet for a sensitive individual working to control health anxiety. How does decaying and putrefying animal flesh nourish and maintain a human herbivore body with its molars on top of each other, smaller mouths, low acid stomach, and longer intestines? Besides, when people choke during a meal, what is the most usual culprit? None other than meat. And if not choked on, meat becomes rotting flesh sliding slowly along at 98 degrees until it is finally and thankfully eliminated from the tube.

Mother's Milk is For Her Baby, Not You

Dairy products, "breast milk" from a cow (or goat or whatever animal is now in vogue to drink from), whether conventional or organic, promote osteoporosis, obesity, cardiovascular disease, as well as breast, prostate, and ovarian cancer, allergies and autoimmune diseases, diabetes, asthma, ulcers, ear and sinus infections, and endometriosis. The milk sugar lactose is broken down into galactose that is toxic to ovarian cells and plays a part in osteoporosis. Dairy products are inflammatory, acid forming, and high in saturated fat and cholesterol that promote cardiovascular disease.

All mammalian breast milk contains the growth hormone IGF-1 (insulin like growth factor-one) that stimulates growth of tissue intended for a sixty pound calf to quickly grow into a 400 pound adult cow or bull within one year. A human adult no longer needs to grow as a child does, making IGF-1 more likely to stimulate tumors to grow. This along with increased estrogen and fifty-nine hormones present in the milk of the pregnant cow further stimulates tissue to grow, grow, grow into tumors.

Cows who are fed synthetic recombinant bovine growth hormone (rBGH) to greatly increase milk production have IGF-1 levels ten times higher than untreated milk. Mastitis—inflammation of the udder—frequently results from cows fed rBGH that are then treated with antibiotics, which end up in the milk as well as the pus from the mastitis. Pus in milk. I can't handle the thought of it.

Dairy further contains pesticides, dioxins, and polychlorinated biphenyls (PCB's) that are all linked to cancer. Heating during pasteurization destroys enzymes, making milk harder to digest and the calcium more insoluble and indigestible. Homogenizing milk breaks down the fat into droplets releasing xanthine oxidase that accumulates on arterial walls leading to heart disease. Cows fed grain rather than grass in CAFO's (inhumane confined animal feeding operations) produce milk deficient in vitamins, minerals, and omega-3's. Most milk and beef contain the bovine leukemia virus (BLV), and in 74 percent of people consuming milk and beef, antibodies for this virus are detected. Even though pasteurization kills this virus, it is not fool proof. Leukemia is twice as prevalent in countries of higher dairy and beef intake, dairy farmers, and other occupations associated with cattle. A study in 2001 found BLV in 10 out of 23 cancerous breast tissue samples (McDougall 2004).

Countries where dairy intake is the highest have the highest osteoporosis and fracture rates. To prevent osteoporosis, decrease salt intake, eat high calcium foods (beans, almonds, greens, sesame seeds, and tofu), and practice weight-bearing exercise in the sun for vitamin D. Plant based sources of calcium are superior to animal based sources, as the calcium in kale and broccoli is absorbed nearly twice as much as the calcium in cow's milk. Avoid tobacco, coffee, and phosphate additives in meat (preservative) and cola (used to keep cola brown). Healthy bones need calcium, vitamin D, magnesium, boron, phosphorus, copper, zinc, and manganese. Green vegetables contain all these nutrients, unlike milk.

A Content Brain

A healthy diet gives great happiness to the brain and has an essential role in the management of anxiety. A low fat, whole food, plant-based (that is largely uncooked) diet is profoundly healing for the body, mind, and soul. An anti-inflammatory diet is the plant-based diet: fruits, vegetables, nuts and seeds, legumes, whole grains, and omega-3 rich foods. Your brain thrives on omega-3 fatty acids, plants, vitamin B12, sunlight, exercise, and a blood pressure not much higher than 110/70. The most powerful healing

Chapter Two: Brain Care

foods alive are green-leafed vegetables such as kale, collards, spinach, bok choy, and arugula. Fruits and vegetables have 100,000 sun-infused phytonutrients working in synergy to provide a healing symphony that no pill can match. You can't push nature into a pill. Here is a thought from the Bible that speaks to this truth: "Then God said, 'I give you every seed bearing plant on the face of the whole earth and every tree that has fruit with seed in it. They will be yours for food. And to all the beasts of the earth and all the birds in the sky and all the creatures that move along the ground--everything that has the breath of life in it--I give every green plant for food'" (Gen. 1:29, 30 NIV). According to Christianity, the plant-based diet is God's intention for us to nourish our bodies. The Bible further illustrates that veering away from plants as our sole source of food leads to disease.

A low fat, whole food, plant-based (that is largely uncooked) diet is profoundly healing for the body, mind, and soul.

Elephants, horses, and gorillas thrive on uncooked plants, getting plenty of protein for their strong bodies and long lives. In fact, they have longer lives than carnivorous animals. We are trained to think we can only get our needs for protein met from animal foods, yet where does the cow, chicken, or pig get their protein? Not from eating other animals. Let's go right to the source of where protein lies: within the plants. For every piece of meat a person craves, there is a plant-based equivalent. There are salads so richly colored they should be painted, bowls of whole grain with nuts and dried fruit, collard wraps stuffed with vegetables, rice and avocado or tahini and beautiful ripe fruit to eat throughout the day. So let's chow down, and what's more, not gain a pound! Love it.

Although cooking involves life-killing high heat that denatures enzymes and destroys vitamin C and B and polyphenols, it also enhances the availability of other nutrients like lycopene. Cooked carrots, spinach, mushrooms, asparagus, cabbage, peppers, and other vegetables provide more antioxidants as carotenoids when boiled, the least destructive method of cooking. However, uncooked plants have remarkable healing properties. Just take a look at the Gerson therapy method and the story of Chris Wark (http://1ref.us/h6), a young man diagnosed with stage four colon cancer, who although was pressured to undergo chemotherapy after surgical removal of the tumor, refused and began a plant-based diet. He lives to this day.

Cooked animal foods or toxic, processed products posing as food have ingredients that slowly kill you: added sugar (high fructose corn syrup), added salt, hydrogenated oils, and animal protein. Whole, organic plants bathe the brain and body with thousands of nutrients while the standard American diet floods the body with saturated fat, cholesterol, uric acid, animal protein, and toxic chemicals and drugs. A plant-based diet is rich in fiber, which brings satiety and helps prevent rogue cells from getting a toehold in the colon (the colonoscopy business thrives on animal-loaded diets that harm the colon, promoting this "early detection" necessity).

A plant-based health and healing diet can only benefit you versus the foodless food of the standard American diet, which is more responsible for disease and death than sedentary behavior, smoking, and alcohol abuse put together. Routine consumption of refined sugar and starch promotes brain atrophy, increases insulin resistance, feeds rogue cells, and leads to fatty liver disease. The SAD puts one at higher risk of anxiety due to its toxicity and malnutrition. A trash diet of processed food is engineered to deliver the "bliss point," the synergy of sugar, salt, and fat creating the most intense taste sensation. These foods stimulate the reward center in the brain with a jolt of endorphins and dopamine just as cocaine does. It tastes explosively pleasurable, provoking obsession for more trash and great difficulty with portion control.

So people keep shoving it down their throats. Remember the potato chip company that stated "…you can't eat just one"? It was no lie. How about apples? Does anyone ever feel out of control and driven to eat ten apples in one sitting? Processed foods are strangely addictive and also used, unbeknownst to the user, to ironically suppress detoxification—signs of toxins being eliminated from the body—as when eating in the middle of the night so one can go back to sleep. Do you think those nocturnal snacks consist of peas and carrots? Who eats peas and carrots in the middle of the night? Common fare of nocturnal and sometimes black out eating usually consists of processed sugar and flour, dairy, maybe some peanut butter. Trash sugar and flour intake increase serotonin levels temporarily and is one reason why people binge on these foodless foods. Opiate like casomorphins in dairy products, highest in cheese, are addictive and designed to keep a calf close to his or her mother (human milk casomorphins have a different composition than bovine casomorphins and are designed for a human baby only). So people just can't stop taking bite after bite. Big

Chapter Two: Brain Care

Sugar is much like Big Tobacco with its political tactics and harm to the body. May the downfall be soon.

Please do not follow what government and mainstream dieticians advise, as these recommendations are inadequate for full brain nutrition. The actual nutrition guideline should be to simply flood the body with plants every day, eating large amounts of fruits and vegetables at every meal. Whole plant carbohydrates, vitamin B's (grains, legumes, potatoes, bananas, greens, seeds), tryptophan (pumpkin seeds, cashews, and bananas) and omega-3 fatty acids (flax seeds, walnuts, soy and chia seeds) are all essential to keep anxiety at bay.

Let's say a word about tryptophan, which is a precursor for serotonin. We are conditioned to think the best sources are turkey and milk, but researchers at MIT dispelled those beliefs about a decade ago. According to Michael Greger MD, tryptophan is present in most animal foods in small quantities and competes with other amino acids for transport across the blood brain barrier so not much actually gets across to the brain. If one instead consumes plant-based sources of tryptophan, insulin takes up non-tryptophan amino acids into the muscles, and tryptophan has less competition to get across the blood brain barrier.

The most essential nutrient we need, however, is water. One can go weeks without any food but only a few days without any water. We live in a polluted world, and our bodies are continually creating metabolic toxins and fending off external toxins that can produce disease if not eliminated efficiently. Water is the medium through which toxins are diluted and expelled from the body through solid waste, breath, sweat, and urine. The brain is 75 percent water and very sensitive to dehydration. Just a 2 percent loss in water that can happen while exercising on a hot day can lead to a dehydrated brain. With any dehydration, the brain shrinks and becomes progressively thick and sluggish with fatigue, headache, and difficulty thinking clearly—all less hospitable to a peaceful state of mind. Hydration helps to calm anxiety and heightens cognitive abilities with neurotransmitters communicating within a watery medium. Caffeine, added salt, alcohol, and many medications dehydrate. To determine how much water to drink each day, divide your weight in two and drink that number of ounces in between meals. Urine should be very pale yellow in color indicating adequate hydration. If drinking water tastes too bland to you, add some lemon, mint or CALM (magnesium powder), which is soothing and tasty.

Who Does Not Love Fat?

Excessive fat consumption, which is when over 20 percent total calories you consume are from fat, diminishes microcirculation and increases blood viscosity with less effectiveness in clearing out waste. Excessive fat is acid forming, and fatty blood increases the risk for insulin resistance and diabetes, fatty liver, weight gain, sluggishness, and headaches. A high saturated fat diet dulls dopamine efficiency, leading to more fat and sugar consumption. Now, omega-3 polyunsaturated fatty acids are essential for brain health and the cardiovascular system, known as the good fats. Omega-3 helps maintain dopamine and serotonin levels, elevates mood and memory, protect brain cells, prevent or lessen cognitive decline, is anti-inflammatory, decreases triglyceride levels, promotes cardiovascular health, and helps prevent tumorous cells. Omega-3 is obtained from ground flax seeds, walnuts, hemp, and chia seeds in the form of alpha-linoleic acid (ALA). ALA is converted into eicospaentanaenoic acid (EPA) and docsahexaenoic acid (DHA), but is impaired if the diet is high in saturated fat. EPA and DHA can also be found in algae, which is where fish get these nutrients (fish is not recommended due to high arachidonic acid, mercury, dioxins, and other toxins). The body needs Omega-3 and Omega-6 to be in the proper ratio. Omega-6 fatty acids should not go higher than 4:1 Omega-3 fatty acids. The SAD is around 25:1 which is pro-inflammatory. Most vegetable oils are high in Omega-6 fatty acids and should be avoided.

Vitamins

What about vitamins? Vitamin D, which is really a hormone produced in the skin by sun exposure, regulates calcium blood levels and bone health, fertility, immunity, endocrine, and nervous system functioning. Vitamin D receptors are found in most tissues of the body, including the brain. An appropriate level of vitamin D can usually be reached by sensible sun exposure and/or taking 2000 units per day to ward off respiratory illness, premature death, and dysphoric states (Greger 2016). Vitamin D further boosts serotonin levels. Especially during cold weather when the sun is less bright for shorter periods during the day, taking a vitamin D supplement helps to prevent flu and flu terror.

The B vitamins nourish nerve cells and increase energy. They are high in sunflower seeds, greens, almonds, beans, mushrooms, and grains. If one maintains a strict plant diet, one must take a vitamin B12 supplement as

Chapter Two: Brain Care 53

well as receive sufficient omega-3 fatty acids to avoid neurodegenerative and cardiovascular damage and premature death.

Grains

The glutenous grains (wheat, rye, barley, and sometimes oats) have come under controversy. On one hand, they have been connected to mental illness, autism, weight gain, celiac disease, and gluten intolerance. And on the other hand, gluten may increase natural killer cells of the immune system and decrease triglyceride levels. A gluten free diet may increase unfriendly intestinal flora increasing infection risk (Greger 2014). All whole grains are rich in fiber, anti-oxidants, minerals, vitamins, lignans, and phenolic compounds (plant components that inhibit carcinogenesis). Those with celiac disease, gluten sensitivity, or wheat allergy obviously need to avoid glutenous grains. Non-gluten grains include buckwheat, millet, quinoa, teff, and some oats. Eat these freely.

When I changed to a largely uncooked low fat plant diet, I felt illuminated with clarity. For the first time in twelve years, I was sleeping deeply, had no need for medications, and felt further sensitivity to that utter Godsend, my intuition. My energy soared and a deep sense of wellbeing began to pervade my mental state. This beautiful gift is so much more valuable than a cheese sandwich, barbequed piece of tri-tip, slab of eggs benedict, or a steaming cup of mocha latte double cappuccino frappe. There is no value for the foods that are killing us.

Herbs

How about calming herbs for anxiety? Yes. Valerian root taken daily or as needed can promote deep sleep and has a strong anti-anxiety component. Valepotriates in valerian bind to the same receptors in the brain that benzodiazepines do. Valerian contains B vitamins and magnesium, producing calmness and the ability to maintain a more sensible perspective. It may be taken with melatonin for sleep enhancement. You can begin at 100 mg/day, though some will find relief in divided doses as high as 1000 mg a day. Other calming herbs include chamomile, lavender oil topically, St John's wort, hops, skullcap, passionflower, and licorice. Cayenne increases endorphins and helps organs to release toxins. This hot herb also opens up arteries that, if atherosclerotic, brings a greater flow of life, preserving blood to the heart and brain as well as other tissue. Garlic helps with nervous disorders. Gotu kola decreases anxiety and increases mental stamina. Hawthorn helps the heart and decreases insomnia and tension. Ashwagandha fortifies the adrenals and protects from adrenal exhaustion.

Dick Quinn in *Left for Dead* wrote of healing his congestive heart failure after a heart attack at age forty-two. A subsequent failed coronary bypass surgery left him very weak, and he was not expected to live. He soon met a woman versed in healing, who directed him to take cayenne pepper. Cayenne dilated his coronary arteries, giving his heart plentiful oxygenated blood and eighteen more years of life. However, he could have had even more years if he had also stopped eating atherosclerotic-promoting meat, which contributed to the abdominal aneurysm that ruptured and killed him at age sixty. This inspiring story illustrates the need for the holistic approach to healing rather than a magic bullet pill approach while other destructive behaviors continue. Believing a magic bullet of exercise or vitamins or herbs or deep tissue massage or psychic consultations will protect you from disease and/or disability despite a destructive lifestyle (i.e. trash diet, habitual drinking, or out of control anger) will at best be effective for a temporary period of time or worse, not work at all. In other words, problem drinking will not be cancelled out by running marathons. Even though none of us can claim perfection while living amidst various toxicities, let us seek the interconnected reality of health beyond tunnel vision.

Fasting

We live in a physically and mentally polluted world: lethal foods, environmental pollutants, agitated sounds, and disturbing sights, information, and images. Avoiding these toxicities is more or less unrealistic, so what do we do? We must live according to a very simple law: health giving nutrients for the mind and body must be taken in while physical and psychic toxins must be purged out. Otherwise sooner or later, various maladies of body and mind will appear. Detoxifying is essential to decongest the body and mind of waste and anxiety. A low fat, plant-based diet, and fasting or cleanses provide this needed purging. The body is self-healing and hardwired to maintain homeostasis. My brain will be content if I give it what it needs as the right fuel, adequate brain rest, and remove from it what it does not need: clearance of its waste and excess acidity.

Let us discuss a cleansing process that detoxifies the brain and body known as fasting. Abstinence from everything except water for more than one day allows the body to release toxins that may be hidden in deep places

Chapter Two: Brain Care

in the body like bones and organs. Poisons and waste in the body include acidic mucus, drugs, toxins, heavy metals, and synthetic chemicals in food. For example, the artificial sweetener aspartame and its breakdown product formaldehyde, which is a known carcinogen used to embalm dead bodies, is a neurotoxin that damages neurons that may result in headaches, brain tumors, numbness, muscle spasms, insomnia, and tinnitus (Mercola 2011). This chemical and many others needs to be thrown out of the body quickly and kept out for good.

Fasting decreases IGF-1, balances blood glucose with increased insulin sensitivity, turns on the fat-burning mode, decreases cholesterol and uric acid levels, and decreases blood pressure. Fasting reboots the immune system by triggering stem cell regeneration of white blood cells helping to heal autoimmune diseases. The body has a large capacity for storing toxins from food, water, or air, placing them in adipose (fat) tissue. The body is protective of that storage, as released toxins flooding the body too abruptly can be harmful to health. This is why people can have difficulty losing weight, especially those last few pounds. Bones store heavy metals (cadmium, mercury, arsenic, lead) that are slowly released when given the chance through a cleansing, plant-based diet and other detoxification practices. When allowed to leave the body, these heavy metals can be irritating to the nervous system, kidneys, liver, heart, and all body tissues. Signs and symptoms may worsen as toxins are being released, bringing discomfort, inflammation, and transient limitation: "I just can't get out of bed." Perhaps one will even vomit or have diarrhea, but these experiences will reveal how toxic your body has been and how good it is to release congestion and harmful substances.

Fasting energizes the mind and loosens habitual negative thinking pathways. A daily fasting period, fourteen to twenty hours, helps to decongest the brain and liver. This daily fasting could begin with not eating anything after an early, low fat dinner and having a late breakfast the next day. Try a 24 hour fast beginning at 3:00 pm and ending at 3:00 pm the next day. There are also cleansing diets involving only raw fruit and vegetables for three to seven days. Helpful foods, such as cabbage, onions, garlic, cilantro, sea vegetables, lemons, and grapefruit, will assist liver detoxification and release waste back into circulation to be eliminated.

Unpasteurized vegetable juice has a tranquilizing effect, as it immediately floods your body with massive phytonutrients and is highly alkalinizing. Vegetable juice is so soothing; it can take the place of a benzodiazepine with its addictive potential and side effects. Many with terminal diseases have regained health by juicing vegetables. Clearing with enemas, sweating, fasting, neti pot sinus cleansing, and whole raw fruit and vegetables help to decongest the liver and help clear the head and brain of congestion (goodbye, migraine horror). Clearing can take weeks, as you give your body a chance to release toxicity by fasting and/or nourishing with plants. Detoxifying can be uncomfortable and prolonged, possibly one of the hardest and healthiest things you ever do, but the rewards are priceless.

Sleep and Jumping Out of Bed

Deep, drug-free sleep preserves emotional and mental health, enhancing memory, learning, creativity, and well-being. Miserable sleep equals miserable anxiety, so let's just fix any sleep problem now. I can speak to this because once I stopped sleeping for a year and felt out of my mind with bafflement and exhaustion. Severe sleep deprivation will end your life faster than food deprivation, and it impairs the brain to the point of paranoia and hallucinations. Less severe sleep deprivation exacerbates anxiety, as it overly stimulates the amygdala and heightens sympathetic nervous system reactivity. Chronic sleep deprivation raises cortisol levels and adrenal fatigue, raises blood pressure, and promotes weight gain, diabetes, and stroke. Ghrelin, the hunger hormone, increases, which tells you to eat until you drop.

Growth hormone, serving to maintain healthy tissue during adulthood, is produced by the pituitary gland and is released during exercise and the first ninety minutes of stage four sleep. Poor sleep decreases growth hormone, leading to anxiety, decreased clarity of thinking, insulin resistance, higher blood fats, and faster aging. During sleep, the body removes toxins and amyloid protein (involved in Alzheimer's disease) from neurons. Tissue repair occurs and inflammation is modulated, homeostasis and circadian rhythm are normalized, and immune integrity is preserved.

As for your circadian rhythm, do you love the morning like a lark or do you thrive during evening and late night hours like an owl? The most restorative sleep is between 10:00 p.m. and 2:00 a.m., which is when the adrenal system recharges and the gall bladder dumps toxins and neurotoxins as aspartame, MSG, aluminum, mercury, and fluoride to be processed by the liver. Those who identify as night owls should still try to fall asleep before 2:00 a.m., as insomnia and staying up into the night leads to serotonin dumping in uncontrolled ways. Morning larks continue your pattern of going to bed early.

Chapter Two: Brain Care 57

Sleep care involves evening rituals as consistently going to bed at the same time, shifting to softer lighting and cessation of provocative stimuli such as screen use, heavy discussion, loud music, and upsetting media information. The pineal gland secretes melatonin, the sleep-inducing hormone made from serotonin, mostly at night, so it is dependent upon softer lighting in the evening to be released into circulation. Avoid being on the Internet after 9:00 p.m., as the computer screen exudes blue lighting, similar to daylight that interferes with melatonin production leading to insomnia. Melatonin regulates one's circadian rhythm and helps prevent diseases such as cancer, depression, dementia, hypertension, and diabetes. We need the right amount of sleep, as sleeping more than nine hours or less than six hours impairs circadian rhythm and is depressogenic.

The common teaching to get seven to nine hours of uninterrupted sleep may not apply to all people. Some cultures have two sleeps: sleep for a few hours, get up and socialize or work, then go back to sleep for a few more hours. A true health-promoting diet and lifestyle frequently results in deeper, more healing sleeps that may result in needing less sleep than one previously required i.e. instead of needing nine hours, six and a half hours is sufficient. A word needs to be said about stressful life situations that can interfere with sleep such as in a job or relationship that feels overwhelmingly bad. Do what you have to: leave it, address it, or pray to be shown the right direction to protect yourself. Sleep will follow. Rule in recovery: sleep or be a wreak.

Routine use of benzodiazepines taken to induce sleep ironically interferes with deep sleep and should be used for the shortest time possible if at all. Nightmares can be brought on by antidepressants that decrease rapid eye movement (REM) of dreaming during deep sleep. Low blood glucose, serotonin, and GABA can cause nightmares and anxiety upon awakening. Melatonin supplements can be helpful for insomnia, but some people experience nightmares with melatonin supplementation. If taken nightly, one should be aware that high doses, greater than one mg, can lead to depression.

Invite life-saving sleep into every bedtime by getting exercise in the sun (without sunscreen) for at least thirty minutes every day. Stay away from foodless foods and nourish yourself with whole plant foods, avoiding late and/or high fat dinners. Short daily fasting and minimizing exposure to toxins can heal insomnia. Tryptophan rich foods, magnesium, as well as valerian and passion flower (calming herbs) promote sleep duration and depth.

Frederick Pierce, an American poet and author (1878-1935), wrote: "Five minutes, just before going to sleep, given to a bit of directed imagination regarding achievement possibilities of the morrow, will steadily and increasingly bear fruit, particularly if all ideas of difficulty, worry or fear are resolutely ruled out and replaced by those of accomplishment and smiling courage."

Bring on the BDNF

Brain derived neurotrophic factor (BDNF) is a protective protein found in the brain and body that acts as fertilizer for neurons, increasing their growth and developing stronger connections with other neurons. This neuroplasticity also works to build either a joyful perspective on life or a defeatist and dysphoric attitude influenced by that on which one focuses. So, if I am filled with dread, self-doubt, and catastrophic thinking while sitting catatonically in a chair, then BDNF will build that negativity, and I will continue to cycle in and out of anxiety. But if I am filled with determination and faith as I leap out of the chair, then BDNF will build healing and happiness. Maintaining adequate levels of BDNF supports cognitive functioning and can pave the way for emotional healing with optimal neurotransmission, helping to prevent mental dysfunction.

The hippocampus is critical in managing associations between stimuli and emotion. Anxiety interferes with the hippocampus connecting stimuli as a new or uncomfortable sensation to neutral, non-alarming emotion, making it difficult to learn new and reasonable connections. The hippocampus is a target for cortisol, which when elevated is neuro-toxic to the memory center, causing it to shrink in size. Anxiety and depression is associated with hippocampal atrophy, but BDNF allows for neurogenesis and neuroplasticity of the hippocampus, breaking its bonds from fear and dysphoria. What decreases this protective protein? Sedentary behavior, isolation, substance abuse (including foodless food), feeling powerless and demoralized, or experiencing chronic stress. Decreased levels of BDNF promote dementia, neurotransmitter dysfunction, and mental illness. There are ways to increase BDNF that promote mental and emotional resilience: intense daily exercise, green tea, a plant-based diet, meditation, healthy friendships, learning a new skill, and spending time in the sun. Unlike an endorphin high from intense exercise, increasing BDNF and subsequent neuroplasticity takes time and consistency. Everyday practice a BDNF boosting activity, and above all, cast doubt on any doom and negativity that a part of you will likely project as that is what it is used to doing.

A Content Tube and Brain Partnership

The whole gastrointestinal system, starting with the mouth, has a brain of its own and is known as the enteric nervous system. This long tube has five hundred million neurons secreting many of the same neurotransmitters as the brain; ninety-five percent of the body's serotonin and a substantial amount of dopamine is produced within this tube. The brain is glad about this arrangement, as the process of digestion is perilous and messy, and the brain has enough to do.

Our gastrointestinal tract also contains 100 trillion bacteria with 1000 different species of friendly and unfriendly bacteria. It is now considered a separate organ with a metabolic capacity exceeding the liver (Greger 2016). This microbiota communicates with the intestinal wall that is linked to the immune, endocrine, and nervous systems. We need a balance of unfriendly to friendly bacteria in a 15 percent to 85 percent ratio to help digest food; make vitamins such as biotin, B12, folate and vitamin K; decrease cancerous cells and other pathogens; reduce inflammation and autoimmunity (body attacking itself); help provide satiety and maintain mental well-being. Some of the bacteria can modify the regulation of neurotransmitters like serotonin and dopamine. Gastrointestinal problems and microbiota imbalance can lead to anxiety and depression as well as inflammatory bowel disease, colon cancer, diabetes, and cardiovascular disease. Consuming inflammatory and processed foods, drugs (including antibiotics, alcohol, caffeine, and nicotine), heavy metals, and meats (i.e. saturated fatty acids), as well as using household and personal products tip the microbiota balance, proliferating unfriendly bacteria. Even stress and feeling overwhelmed can increase unfriendly bacteria.

Prebiotics are the fiber in plant foods. Jerusalem artichokes, onions, garlic, leeks, mushrooms, beans, cruciferous vegetables, bananas, almonds, radishes, and apples feed friendly bacteria, which produce a short chain fatty acid known as butyrate. Butyrate, in turn, feeds the cells lining the colon. This decreases carcinogenic cells, inflammation, and leaky gut, all while increasing BDNF and plasticity. It also helps prevent autoimmune illnesses, strengthening the immune system, all while decreasing cholesterol and atherosclerosis. The microbiota runs on fiber and is what our good bacteria love. Exercise and fermented foods, such as miso and tempeh, also increase friendly and diverse bacteria.

Part of the friendly microbiota is an opportunistic yeast that helps to detect and destroy other pathogenic bacteria and control blood sugar levels. Called candida albicans, it is ordinarily kept in balance by friendly bacteria, but with stress, a trash diet, antibiotics, and alcohol, candida morphs into friendly yeast gone wild and becomes an invasive filamentous fungus that can cause problems as fatigue, weight gain, joint pain, gas, sore throat, headache, abdominal pain, anxiety, and depression. Poor food combinations, as in any type of sugar combined with fat, leads to overgrowth of candida, increased blood sugar levels, insulin resistance, and decreased immunity. Avoiding this combination of fat and sweets as well as keeping total fat intake to 20 percent or less, improves energy, digestion, mood, sleep, and helps to reverse degenerative disease. Treatment for candida overgrowth includes oregano oil, coconut, garlic, and hydrochloric acid, which you supplement with meals.

This is why it is essential to have an intact and non-inflamed intestine with balanced microbiota fed by whole plant foods, free of chemicals and drugs that damage essential friendly bacteria and promote inflammation. There is no doubt that a healthy and contented body thrives upon a plant-based diet, stress composure, and avoidance of toxic chemicals.

Stand Up Straight and Breathe: The Vagus Nerve

The vagus nerve, the "nerve of compassion," is a long, wandering nerve beginning in the brainstem and traveling deeply into the abdomen sending parasympathetic messages to the brain, throat, larynx, lung, diaphragm, heart, spleen, organs of digestion, kidney, female reproductive organs, ears, and tongue. This great nerve also tells the brain how everything in the trunk is doing. It is the main nerve of the PSNS, giving rise to the rest-and-digest state versus the fight-or-flight reaction of the sympathetic nervous system. The vagal neurotransmitter, acetylcholine, is an anti-stress neurotransmitter (please know that mercury, so high in fish, impairs its functioning). The vagus nerve is largely responsible for the mind-body connection. Therefore, we need strong vagal tone to help control anxiety.

What weakens vagal tone may also result from weak vagal tone: injury to the vagus nerve i.e. whiplash or surgery, sleep deprivation and fatigue, anxiety and depression, chronic stress, pain, and histamine intolerance. Digestive distress (hiatal hernia, heavy meals, or backed up stool, etc.) that irritates and puts pressure on the vagus nerve may lead to shortness of breath, palpitations, headache, dizziness, and fainting (the vaso-vagal response, due to bradycardia, slowing of the pulse). Other vagal irritants include poor posture and muscular imbalances, alcohol and drugs, an imbalanced microbiota and overly spicy food. These irritants make the vagus nerve less effective in sending calming, parasympathetic messages.

Chapter Two: Brain Care

This produces a myriad of symptoms from more anxiety and/or depression with increased emotional liability, gastrointestinal upsets, increased heart rate, fatigue, brain fog, depersonalization, chronic pain, tinnitus, esophageal inflammation and spasms, heartburn, hiatal hernia, gastritis, insomnia, palpitations, startling easily, chest fullness, abdominal pain, nausea, stomach spasms, irritable bowel syndrome, bitter taste, eating disorders, shortness of breath, headaches, and dizziness. The vagal nerve may also become overactive, misfiring in reaction to ordinary stimuli resulting in fainting, hiccups, or diarrhea. This is why, for some, the sight of blood leads to fainting.

The brain and gastrointestinal system are inextricably linked with the gut sending signals to the brain via the vagus nerve while the gut listens to the brain's emotional state. This is why stress nearly always leads to gastrointestinal discomforts, and conversely, when the gut is inflamed or congested, it sends messages of dysphoria to the PFC and limbic system. When your gut is upset, it equals your brain being upset and vice versa. Strong vagal tone between gut and brain not only promotes stress resilience but also control of appetite and satiety.

Anxiety causes shallow, rapid breathing that stokes the sympathetic nervous system, which only heightens anxiety and creates more shallow rapid breathing. This can lead to numbness, tingling, light-headedness, a constricted chest, increased heart rate, and a feeling of suffocation. The blood becomes more alkaline, which constricts blood vessels and leads to less oxygen to the brain, causing dizziness and feelings of unreality. Taking five to six longer breaths per minute while counting to three inhaling and to five exhaling and expanding the belly, slows the heart rate and even prevents panic attacks. It is interesting to know that the vagus nerve keeps the heart rate between sixty to eighty bpm. Otherwise, the SNS would have it going around 100 bpm, and the heart would wear out faster with more risk for cardiac events.

The next time a panic attack occurs, tell the attack that a panic attack never lasts more than a few seconds and that you can handle it. You absolutely can handle it, though panic is so painful. Although stress releases stress hormones that override the PSNS, deep and slow breathing strengthens the vagus nerve that restores calmness and decreases sympathetic nervous system (SNS) arousal, facilitating rewiring of the brain with new pathways of serenity and fortitude. The brain can then calm itself more fully.

Stop now and notice your breathing. Is it shallow or full, rapid or slow? How is your posture? Slumped with your head jutting forward? Straighten you head and back with chest open, and take a deep breath, breathing out any tension you might feel. Because anxious thoughts can be ruminative and percussive, meeting each anxious impulse with short exhalation bursts can prevent the anxious thought from gaining a foothold in one's mind. Breathing and posture matter, as these help the frontal lobe catch up to an emotional alarm reaction. Your frontal lobe can then fully understand what is happening and then mount a rational response. Therefore, when strong emotion hits, breathe, stand tall, then respond. Practice deep breathing at least twice a day and as needed, releasing all health alarms that you suspect may be coming from a dramatic amygdala.

Visceral feelings and gut instincts are emotional intuitions sent up to your brain via the vagus nerve. These intuitions modulate mood and anxiety, and they facilitate unlearning a conditioned fear response (Bergland 2014). When working to expose and extinguish a fear-trigger sensation, such as shooting head pain or a cramping colon, belly breathing augments re-connecting the fear-trigger to a neutral response: "A shot of pain. This too shall pass." The vagus nerve instinct is very sensitive to mental activity and social non-verbal expressions and is worthy of being trusted. Become quiet and centered enough through prayer and meditation to hear the deeper message from the gut telling the brain that there are no worries to be had.

Strong vagal tone brings compassion and exuberance, while amplifying intuitive messages. Vagal tone is also enhanced by living in accordance with one's circadian rhythm, healthy eating, happy friendships and marriages, laughter, exercise and yoga, cold water facial splashes or cold showers, massage, singing, fasting, acupuncture, an optimistic attitude, and daily habits that bring contentment into your life. As Bergland writes, this strong tone works to maintain grace under pressure that helps to overcome fear-conditioning.

A Little Blue Zone

The body is magnificently designed to manifest radiant, everlasting health if given the right nutrients, exercise, and mental attitude. The river of life, the blood stream, nourishes cells promoting clarity of mind, as the brain is also bathed in this river. We should do what we can to keep this river free from chemicals that our bodies don't recognize and struggle to metabolize, which only stresses the liver and kidneys and irritates the brain. Let us consume the healing power of plants to protect our health, and let us clear the body of trash with fasting or consuming fruits and

Chapter Two: Brain Care

vegetables only for a few days. Some brain care needs are universal such as making plant foods the mainstay of our diet and avoiding trans fats, refined sugar/starch, grilled and processed animal flesh, synthetic chemicals, and dairy. That way of eating is harmful for everyone. A gene for disease is the bullet, and a less than optimal lifestyle is what pulls the trigger.

The "Blue Zones" denote areas in the world where people are known to live very long and healthy lives, up to 100 years or longer. They include such places as Okinawa, Japan; Nicoya, Costa Rica; Icaria, Greece; and Loma Linda, California, USA. The blue zone people are often physically active, have strong communities, and eat largely plant-based diets with none or very little meat or dairy. Rather than being found in a remote, romantic village under towering mountains where people live a primitive lifestyle, we can easily become our own little blue zone by adopting a simple lifestyle of a plant-based diet, daily exercise, and gratitude for what is truly important: the grace of God bringing the shining sun, kind people, and beloved animals, for instance. With this obtained, one can walk around beaming "I am a blue zone!"

Care of the brain is fundamental in healing health anxiety. Choices and activities that support the brain facilitate new brain pathways and strengthen the pre-frontal cortex of the frontal lobe to stay in charge and calm the limbic system when it becomes overwhelmed and alarmed. Any fear-reducing technique that neglects brain care is transient, at best, in providing relief. No quick, isolated fixes like medication, supplements, or a self-help course will transform this anxiety disorder. Body, mind, and soul together is a powerful healing fortress.

Chapter Three:
Mind Care

Let us ask: when hit by anxiety, are we able to think reasonably? The answer is usually no. In fact, maybe never. Anxiety is volatile; it crowds out reasoning and paralyzes the thinking circuit of the frontal lobe. Chronic anxiety keeps the fear circuits going and interferes with living a life of vivacity and success. The aim of mind care is being able to keep a grip on reasonable thinking that is free from anxiety taking over and mutinying the mind. We need to maintain this grip since health anxiety comprises a four-headed Medusa of physical sensitivities, distorted thinking, emotional leap frogging, and spiritual distress and longing.

Health anxiety involves trigger sensations, such as a cramp, a new freckle, or fleeting light-headedness, that are interpreted through the brain's fear circuit. It seems an impossibility of reining in this distressing and, at times, oppressive circuit. Although we may gain insight into an anxiety episode… "I still can't accept her loss," this insight fails to remedy persisting attacks of anxiety. We continue to contemplate why these attacks persist, trying to identify the culprit: "My body! No, it's my mind! Wait. My mind wouldn't go crazy if my body were not so reactive. My body would be less reactive if my mind would stay calm!" Healing health anxiety recovers the freedom to think about health realistically by retraining the brain to have a rational relationship with thoughts regarding health. Thought management prevents slipping into catastrophic, intrusive, and reactionary thoughts while dismantling destructive beliefs. For example: "Bad things will probably happen without warning! Life is mostly unsafe!" Or "I am having a ceaseless itch. Maybe something is terribly wrong! Maybe I am that one in a thousand with malignant itch syndrome!" We overestimate perceptions as dangerous and catastrophize sensory information, which develops a thinking bias that neglects considering simple and benign alternatives. Distorted thoughts then become the dominating reality in a vicious circle leading to immobility, escalating anxiety, and bleak qualm.

Life experiences and cultural values also influence beliefs and attitudes about health, death, illness, or how robust or fragile I see my body. One's level of health is viewed as either having an inner source ("Health is my responsibility, so I'd better eat well and go for a run") or an outer source ("This problem I have is genetic. We are all so different and there is nothing I can do about it"). Having a strong conviction in an outer, random cause of health or disease leaves room for health anxiety to come roaring down on one like an avalanche, as anxiety is exacerbated by uncertainty. What's more is that self-care is not likely to become a high priority.

Anxiety disorders involve pain-filled thoughts that repeatedly travel and habituate towards brain disaster nerve pathway ruts. Ruminating on these intrusive thoughts feeds them, increasing their frequency and intensity. Furthermore, repetitive thought ruts have a kindling effect where a worrisome thought begins to ignite out of control, and unless reasonably processed, it roars forward exponentially causing a bonfire of worry, fear, exhaustion, and misery. The amygdala overly scrambles to protect one from possible harm that a trigger sensation is imagined to cause. Even though that risk might be one in a hundred, thousand, or million, the amygdala jumps anyway. Thinking with the pre-frontal cortex of the frontal lobe in charge liberates that trigger sensation from automatically traveling down the catastrophic interpretation circuit. Instead, it is directed into the likely probability of it being another benign and maybe uncomfortable manifestation of heightened sensitivity. Recognizing the link between sensations and ineffective, primitive thinking patterns is a first step in building resistance towards slipping into sickness obsession. Separating just enough to witness, instead of being engulfed by, the fear loop creates space to more readily access reasonable thinking. One learns to redirect oneself from obsessing about health. Plato wrote, "Attention to health is the greatest hindrance to life." I would say obsession with health is that hindrance.

Each unreasonable cause of worry seems so real to people who are stuck in anxiety and have lost sight of reasons why it is safe not to worry. They need help to get out of the fear rut just like a car stuck in a ditch needs help to resume moving forward. Besides, the car wants to get out of the ditch and drive on. Containing worry allows the brain to do its work without spinning its wheels in the ditch. The neurochemistry and structural nerve pathway abnormalities involved in anxiety disorders (and other mental maladies) can be remedied with thinking skills and behavior modification. Having an anxiety disorder is not written in stone but is rather like a wild, galloping horse that can be tamed or a thick fog that can be unclouded and dissipated.

A health anxiety attack is comprised of unreasonable intensity of fear: a somatic observation is seen, felt, heard, smelled, or tasted, and suddenly you remember someone who vaguely had the same symptom as you now have who ended up dying. Or maybe a dire medical warning you read from an article, listing signs and symptoms that suddenly sound like yours. These fears can be so unrealistic; they can even take on a hallucinatory quality: "Do I see a strange swelling in my throat? Did I just see red in my stool?? Did my heart just beat strangely? What about my breathing, am I short of breath?" This fleeting illusionary cognitive distortion pushes one into a nose-dive straight into "What if!" reactivity. The conviction of probably being terminal sets in, the adrenals gush out stress hormones, and you start to sweat. Yet, the remedy for this hallucinatory question is going back to a $1+1=2$ reality: place your hand in front of your face. Do you see it? Apply this reality test to any questions of exactly what are you seeing. Am I asking a question or am I seeing a perception? If you find yourself asking versus experiencing a clear cut perception the answer is NO, I am not seeing or feeling something threatening. Rule for recovery: unless I clearly perceive something unsafe, I will let the illusion and doubt go.

Discernment: A Finely Tuned Brain

You can learn to sense a true problem from a benign somatic expression, uncomfortable as it may be, even though you have not had extensive medical training. You may still educate yourself with study, intuition, and trusted, professional assistance. I found that being a nurse was both a blessing and a curse: I possessed enough information to place terrifying labels on a sensation or observation but then had enough knowledge

Chapter Three: Mind Care

to rule out bad diagnoses and calm irrational thinking. This duplicitous thinking is circuitous and futile of which a finely tuned brain can overcome.

Disease is unequivocally disturbing while benign conditions have a limited, sometimes hidden softness and/or familiarity to them. For example, a large breast cyst is round and buoyant versus the usual hard roughness of a bad tumor. Some benign conditions can be intensely uncomfortable as in migraine headaches or the trigger points of fibromyalgia, which can be intermittent and move around. We come to know these pains well. Obviously high fevers, profuse bleeding, seizures, chest pain with shortness of breath and lightheadedness, nausea, altered states of consciousness, and other emergencies require medical assistance.

The sensitive body expresses its struggle with toxicity in a louder manner than the next person. While the increased stress hormone norepinephrine magnifies a sensation, making it harder for the left brain to recognize the reason for the sensation, ask the sensation "Sensation, have we met before? What is your message for me?" Simultaneously, assert routinely, "I will notice a true problem. I have healing tools, and I am safe." Listen to and trust what your body has to say. This solid assertion is the lucid truth of foundational, reasonable thinking that keeps the brain's relationship to anxiety manageable and appropriate.

A well cared for brain is able to sense the body without misinterpreting and magnifying sensations and observations. Less static is heard as the brain and body are in greater brain wave harmony and frontal lobe integrity. A chaotic and unhappy brain makes it difficult to evaluate sensations and reach a rational understanding of the various manifestations that the body creates. This agitated state promotes a negative bias when processing sensory information and pursuing safety behavior. Once, I obsessed about a birthmark mole for an entire year. Moles can itch and become inflamed; they can also lose pigmentation as they age with different shades of color i.e. pinkish and brown similar to one of the dreaded warning signs of skin gone wrong. I had connected medical warnings of "mole color differences" and turned into a fear lunatic about my own little mole. Obsessively scanning this mole, it seemed to say to me "I am innocent! Stop this obsessing about me and leave me in peace!" I did leave the poor mole in peace, and it remains contentedly on my leg, healthy and innocent, even today. These changes are benign and within normal variations of health throughout a day or within decades.

Why Health Anxiety is Confounding

I found that recovering from panic disorder was easier than health anxiety, as panic has less of a margin of reality testing and is less convoluted. I quickly learned the swift rise and fall of a panic attack: "Suddenly I feel detached from reality! Am I going to scream or collapse and die in public?!........OK, I am OK now. I can breathe again." Objects of fear such as bridges, elevators, heights, or insects are outside of ourselves and are more definitive: "There is an insect flying. This is crazy!" It is true that an elevator could get stuck or a bridge could crumble in an earthquake, but these risks remain outside of ourselves and are more mechanical. A phobia has well-defined edges of itself, while health anxiety merges and creeps into rational health knowledge. This interferes with the mind gaining momentum towards identifying the edges of the health fear. Many times behavioral conditioning, breathing, and relaxing through a hierarchy of fear-inducing experiences, such as a bridge or elevator, is sufficient to heal these phobias.

The complexity of health anxiety may be viewed with an analogy: health anxiety is to phobias as food addiction is to alcoholism. A phobia based in an improbable reality (i.e. driving and running over someone) is less complex to zero in on and work through. It is similar to recovery with alcoholism that begins with simply not picking up that first drink. With food addiction, one must continue to eat, and at the same time practice food sobriety with more variables to negotiate, such as when, what or quantity to eat. Some aspects of food addiction are more clear cut, such as refined sugar and starch, and are consciously avoided. Personal binge foods, such as chips, cheese, and chocolate, are also avoided. With health anxiety, one must continue to take care of and monitor one's body: gaining some basic knowledge of health fundamentals, learning how to react sanely to a health sensation/situation, separating oneself from irrational health anxiety thoughts and images, and figuring out when to seek assistance—kind, trusted, and appropriate assistance.

Health anxiety is complex and difficult to treat because the object of this type of anxiety springs from the body, and it can have an infinite amount of expressions, functions, and potential problems. Health concerns are within the realm of possibility, unlike a psychotic delusion of believing an electronic transmitter has been planted in your ear from another galaxy or that you have two hearts beating inside of your chest. These delusions are outside the realm of possibility.

Chapter Three: Mind Care

In most types of somatic symptom and related disorders that are marked by excessive body vigilance, thoughts of health risks can be entwined with the goals of self-image (ego-syntonic) such as when someone has an unshakeable belief in a health condition that does not exist. Or alternatively, health thoughts can be in conflict with one's self-image (ego alien) as in unwanted thoughts (ego-dystonic state): "This is a crazy waste of time to keep thinking about this ingrown toe, growling belly, or if my swallowing is normal." But, "Am I experiencing irrational fear or do I have a valid concern?" Health fears flip from ego syntonic thoughts: "Wait, no. This does look strange. Didn't I read something about ... I have got to take care of my health!" to ego-dystonic painful thoughts: "Not this thought again! I already processed this thought, and here it is again, like a song I don't even like, going over and over in my head! I tell you, I am fine!"

Ego-syntonic and dystonic thinking can merge so quickly that it can be difficult to determine where one ends and the other one starts: "Not this thought again! But, wait!" It's enough to make your head spin. This back and forth between submerging into the fear and recognizing the irrationality of the fear interferes with getting a foothold in the logical conclusion: "Ok! Not going to go there! I know this is senseless anxiety, and I am gone!" Assessing somatic perceptions requires added mental processing to 1) recognize harmlessness or something needing more attention as with an infection and 2) separate perceptions from irrational thinking. There should not be too much added processing, as the quick slide into obsession is baffling and powerful. "I will not fail to notice something significant—boom—done!" The lurking uncertainty and insistence of anxiety goading "yes, but this fear is in the realm of possibility" is very strong, but you still have to embrace recovery tools and go forward. Just forget the realm of possibility while you bravely go ahead and state: "This is not me; it's my health anxiety kicking up just like a mule." Conversely, do you spend a lot of time thinking what you would do if you won the lottery? Why not? This is in the realm of possibility as well. Constant worries about health are equally a waste of time and harmful to mind, body, and soul.

Nearly every fear involves a margin of reality testing. With health anxiety, there is a large margin of reality testing. The left and right brain come together to rein in this margin of reality testing. Ok, then, what did they say about: moles, coughs, cysts or dizziness? A pre- or post-menopausal woman can have a chronically irritated throat secondary to decreased estrogen levels. Cysts can be common in a breast, sometimes getting as big as a small grape. Dizziness? Well, the inner ear gets irritated too. Intuition plays its part in reducing this margin with its wisdom and higher knowing. Both of these functions tell you that you are healthy and safe with an unmistakable sensation of certainty that makes the fear vanish. Love it.

A subset of health anxiety, emetophobia (fear of vomiting), is in the realm of possibility for an imperfect body. But why do people throw up? The body is protecting itself from offenders, which is a good thing. Reality testing would look like: have I drunk a large amount of alcohol? Have I eaten at a fast food restaurant or consumed any animal products? Was I recently around someone with the flu? No? Then I will practice thought stopping and thought replacement to cease this rumination of vomiting out of the blue. Negative thought stopping and positive thought replacement with reasonable and uplifting thoughts retrains brain pathways. Switch, switch, switch, and keep switching from dysfunctional thoughts to reasonable and positive thoughts. Stay on the course, and keep retraining your mind, despite strong doubts and a sense of failure. Buck this defeatism and tell yourself, "It is working! I'm not hopeless! I am winning!"

Still, fear is fear. We hear of other people getting sick, even dying. We hear bad health news or stories, and boom, the fear cycle is initiated again. We feel powerless and terrified, caught in the circular rut of "What if?" thinking that goes round and round in our brains, deepening the rut. Yes, anything can happen, but is that my focus? Think of common risky activities and situations: driving a car, being at your job, going on a trip, eating food, exercising, walking across the street, shopping, etc. Let us ask then, are you afraid of driving a car? No? Why not? Do you demand invulnerability every time you get into the driver's seat? Sounds kind of ridiculous, eh? How about flying in a plane? Notice that there is less perceived control with flying; that's what makes fear of flying common. Yes, some people are nervous drivers, but they still get in the car. They may even drive you mad with back seat driving. If, for example, you can get in your car and drive amidst the true possibility of morbidity/mortality, then you are able to recognize that living in a body poses more (think rotten eating) or less (think plant-based diet) of a risk as well. The problem lies in the magnification and obsessing on the remote possibility of a bad thing happening. Strengthening the PFC: "I am going to the store now, period" gets the obsession out of the ACC: "I am going to the store now. But what if someone hits me on the way? Maybe this is a warning! I don't think I should go!" The anxious brain is like a prosecuting attorney, gathering together hits of indictment to build the leverage of the need to consider the fear: being hit by a car while driving is within the realm of possibility. The real problem though is that there is not enough strength in the PFC

Chapter Three: Mind Care

to stand up to this indictment and tell it to "Get away from me, I am going to the store."

What about fearing one disease over another—is this true for you? First, list characteristics of that specific disease that stand out for you. For example: the disease of emphysema might be connected to suffocation, choking, and an extremely painful exit out of life, as every cell screams for a breath of oxygen. These characteristics reflect aspects of yourself that remain overwhelming and unresolved. Do you feel a sense of suffocation in your life? Do you feel doomed and cornered as though life is a claustrophobic net entrenching you? How deep can you go with these connections? How far back can you go? They lie in the essence of you, as you have experienced and lived your life for better or for worse. See these connections in your mind, and then see an angel by your side protecting you. There is something higher with us all the time. Second, pretend that the illness you fear most is the same as the illness you fear less. For example, my health anxiety focused on rogue cells out of control (malignancy), yet I never have had fear of the number one killer: cardiovascular disease. Stories of others my age and gender experiencing heart attacks or strokes do not set off my fear loop amidst knowing that the first symptom can be sudden death. Sudden death! Suddenly it's all over. Woo. Still, I am not afraid of heart disease. I cherish my loyally beating heart perched in my chest, dancing its beat with thousands of mitochondria in each cardiac cell. If I continue to take care of my heart, it will be happy and keep sending every cell in my body the oxygen and nutrients that they love so much. For the rest of my life. Thank you, dear heart. Thank you, dear God, for my heart.

Please take a moment to write down what comprises your own loop of fear and catastrophic irrationality. Think of what triggers you: a certain illness, an illness-related memory, death, new sensations, the media and medical information, or voyeuristic conversations that hype up the latest person's sudden illness. These triggers may be compounded by experiences and beliefs, as a history of traumatic experiences, superstition, self-condemnation, suffering injustice, having a highly sensitive mind/body, or feeling the overwhelming spiritual pain of the immense suffering in the world can weigh us down. Other contributing stressors may involve excess work, impulsive behaviors, excessive screen time, poor daily pacing, questionable people, full moon/solar flares, and poor sleeping.

Write down where you feel this fear loop is going off in your body, whether it be the abdomen, head, throat, jaw, or lower hip—anywhere. Next, write down the intensity of fear felt with various sensations such as having difficulty swallowing, seeing a spot, having a bad headache or transient blurry vision on a scale from one to ten, with ten being the most intense fear. Describe your fear loop with as much detail to gather insight and objective awareness of this loop. Then write down whatever helps you to manage, even flee the fear: health knowledge, talking with someone, medication, time, prayer, or distracting yourself with another activity. Putting all these connections and descriptors down on paper is a necessary first step that can help you recognize and detach from this fear loop. Writing can stop ruminative thinking, as you regain clarity that continues down your arm and hand and then is deposited on the paper.

Safety Behaviors. Not.

Catastrophic health thinking begins with a trigger sensation followed by a fear attack.

Catastrophic health thinking begins with a trigger sensation followed by a fear attack. This stimulus-response conditions the brain, forming a negative thinking bias when processing sensory information. Underneath this fear attack may lurk a superstition that this fear needs appeasing by bowing down to its antics with frantic safety behaviors. The transient relief obtained from performing these safety behaviors hijacks the brain's reward system: "If I run to an expert, she/he will tell me I am OK, and relief will flood over me!" Chasing reassurance, such as checking and re-checking your body and checking with people or medical sites, is a habit-trap formed in the brain's basal ganglia—where panic, fear of being judged, being startled easily, and predicting the worst stems from. This habit is then etched into neural circuitry to be repeated without resolve. The fear habit is now learned and entrenched; the reward of relief that cascades through the mind-body is overwhelmingly soothing, but in that moment, the mind forgets that this relief is always fleeting. One comes to seek these moments of relief near addictively, and it rapidly becomes a negative threat-based habit, which dominates the struggle with health anxiety and interferes with earning trust in one's PFC thinking skills, never to realize the difference between self-care versus reactive obsessing about one's body. Contrarily, a reward-based habit would result from the elation of successfully managing an anxiety attack by utilizing inner skills

Chapter Three: Mind Care

rather than running to the Internet, a book or a person, professional or not, for reassurance and relief.

Unabated health anxiety leads to compulsive safety behaviors designed to escape the anxiety. The problem is that engaging in these safety behaviors is to of no avail in the long run. Reacting to irrational anxiety with denial, the fight-or-flight reaction, or compulsive safety behaviors proves futile. This checking business ironically increases rumination and compulsive behavior as you desperately wait for reassurance. Over and over! One may scour medical media to solve health bafflements, but this frantic searching heightens the obsession with the what, how, and why of the manifestation while the stress hormone cortisol rises and the mood regulator serotonin decreases, impairing clear thinking further.

Let's look further at safety behaviors that seek reassurance:

1. It is common for people with health anxiety to consult doctors with or without getting a multitude of tests. In reality, the body is capable of many mysterious expressions that a doctor may or may not be able to explain. In reality, the body may develop indolent tissue that is labeled as diseased, but it is not. Chasing after doctors for reassurance insists that the answer is outside of ourselves and neglects the fact that the medical system is not fail-safe. In 2012, the New England Journal of Medicine reported that from 1978 to 2008, 1.3 million breast cancer cases detected through mammography were not cancer at all but rather ductal carcinoma in situ that rarely, if ever, progresses to cause harm, and they should be reclassified as benign lesions of epithelial origin with the word carcinoma deleted (Bleyer and Welch 2012). Ironically, mammograms blast the breasts with carcinogenic x-ray wavelengths in order to find cancer early.

"Encapsulated follicular variant of papillary thyroid carcinoma" is another example of a benign nodular growth that has a very low risk of adverse outcome and should be termed "noninvasive follicular thyroid neoplasm with papillary-like nuclear features" to avoid unnecessary thyroid lobe removal and radioactive iodine ablation (Nikiforov, et al 2016). As for prostate screening, PSA (prostate specific antigen) tests may show an elevated PSA level, which can occur in other conditions that affect the prostate such as prostate enlargement, infection, medication, recent use of a catheter or scope, riding a bike, frequent ejaculation, or increasing age. Some prostates just make more PSA than others. A biopsy may reveal low or high-grade prostatic intraepithelial neoplasia (PIN). If low, no further treatment is necessary, and it is virtually indistinguishable from benign tissue. However, PIN can lead to needless surgeries, treatment, and anxiety. Even people who don't have health anxiety greatly dislike this cancer word hanging over them. Screening and over diagnosis has not resulted in decreased mortality, so something is not working. And does anyone realize this? CT scans are massively high tech x-rays that expose the body to hundreds of times more radiation than regular x-ray, the same as smoking 700 cigarettes. One-fifth to one-half of CT scans are unnecessary (Greger 2015).

This is not to infer that all medical doctors are unscrupulous and to stay away from them. This is only to encourage people not to reflexively collapse into assuming this system will automatically fix a health problem. Medicine is a very powerful and hypnotic business with huge technology that glamorizes it. Its linear focus is on treating outer causes and relieving symptoms and less so on creating radiant and long lasting healing at the core. True healing with a plant-based diet and other natural options is not as profitable as symptomatic treatment. Over $100 billion per year is spent on chemotherapy, which is highly toxic. Absolutely, the medical system does save lives with certain emergency and surgical interventions. But the fact remains that more than 300,000 Americans die every year from (properly) prescribed prescriptions, wrong medication, hospital errors, hospital acquired infections, unnecessary surgery, and surgical complications. Healthcare has now risen to the third cause of death in America (Greger 2015).

It is unfortunate that unscrupulous physicians exist. One doctor reported to me that I had an aortic bruit (abnormal sound) and probable aneurysm (I am slender and my smooth, intact and non-bulging aorta is heard loudly). An ENT stated I had a "thickening" in my chest x-ray seven years prior, yet the radiologist savvy ER physician read it as "perfectly healthy." Another physician looked at me gravely upon learning my diet was plant-based. She worriedly began listing all the lab tests I needed to measure the many deficiencies she imagined a plant-diet caused. A urologist directed me to schedule a cystoscopy (tube up urethra and into bladder to diagnose a bladder condition) with a strange look in his eye, and he later made many attempts to get me back into his office for this unneeded procedure. Had he not heard of interstitial cystitis?

The culmination of inner healer clarity came for me when, after ten years of yearly throat hemorrhaging, I finally discovered the diagnosis of this benign and rare disorder. No doctor or specialist ever diagnosed me with angina hemorrhagic bullae. I did. Got it, I concluded, no more running to these clinicians when anxious about my health in an attempt to squash the knee-jerk fear. Forget about it. I would have to become my

Chapter Three: Mind Care

own healer. As awesome as medical doctors can be in emergencies, they are often not educated to heal but only to treat problems with drugs and surgery. They do not heal the underlying cause of many non-emergency problems. Sometimes a doctor will break free from the medical/drug regime to practice true healing with plants and lifestyle changes. Think of Dr. Michael Greger, Dr. Suzanne Humphries, Dr. John McDougall, Dr. Joel Fuhrman, Dr. T. Colin Campbell, Dr. Max Gerson, and Dr. Neal Barnard to name a few.

Have only one caregiver whom you trust. Visit this caregiver only after doing a reality check to make sure the reason for going is valid rather than crazed and obsessive. Those frantic office visits further undermine one's connection and trust with one's inner and higher Healer, an essential part of recovery.

2. It is also common for one to repeatedly scan medical information in an attempt to try to convince the right brain that there is no need to worry. "Cyberchondria" describes going berserk while reading infinitely terrifying medical information on various medical sites. With a smartphone, you can scan any symptom anywhere and anytime: in the bathroom, in the car, while you are shopping. No! Researching the media for health reassurance exacerbates obsessive focusing upon a sensation as catastrophic, and it increases anxiety in the long run instead of alleviating it. Informative as medical information may be at times (a lead that provides temporary relief and spurs on the chase), it is sterile in its delineation of various diseases that can either provide transient relief or escalate worry into panic.

The media can contribute to health anxiety, as it often portrays illness as obscure and possibly right around the bend. When researching medical sites, one may find that they may not list simple and/or benign reasons for a sensation or perception. Neither is it mentioned that the probability of that perception being dangerous is low. Low! The preoccupation with disease risk is then reinforced. Granted, searching the Internet sometimes does give teaching and understanding, as for example, "This is just an esophageal spasm!" Yet this isolated reassurance does not solve the fear problem. Approaching medical information must be done from a centered, rational mental posture. If a mysterious sensation leads to an effort to understand it further, one should begin with the simplest of explanations. So if you have chapped lips, do not research lip cancer. Look up dry lips first and then tell your amygdala: "Ya see?" Immediately looking up a worst-case scenario stems from catastrophic thinking and is considered compulsive behavior. Stop it, now! From now on, it is forbidden. Rule in recovery: no more diving into worst-case scenarios.

Much of mainstream medical information is in reaction to the mainstream way of life that almost always involves a destructive lifestyle as a carnivorous diet, alcohol use, chemically laden personal products, and inadequate exercise. When one practices a plant-based lifestyle, one is no longer part of this collective risk and illness pool that modern medicine focuses on diagnosing and treating. For example, it is thought that kidney function naturally declines with age, yet the truth is that the chronic acid load of meat and dairy products as well as an increased ammonia production to buffer this acidic load causes kidney tubular toxicity and damage. So you can daringly state that most of the medical culture does not apply to you! Reflect now on what place the medical system have in society if most people were plant-based and walked, ran, swam, and danced? Instead, the pharmaceutical-medical industry is a multi-billion-dollar industry, and cardiovascular disease—a disease of lifestyle—is the number one killer, raking in a whole pack of cash. Fear tactics found in literature and the media seem to be designed to continue funneling would-be patients into this system and maintaining the status quo.

3. Many people with health anxiety talk with others secretly scanning for reassurance. When speaking with others who don't experience or understand health anxiety, one may react with frustration when they say, "I'm not a doctor, just go get it checked!" Waiting…and checking! The dreaded waiting room and the dreaded waiting to hear the results—what a combination for going over the edge. Feeling helpless themselves, others with health anxiety may avoid bringing this topic up in the future. We hide the embarrassment and shame of talking to someone, trying to sound nonchalant and casual as we scan with hyper vigilance: "Have you ever had anything like this?" We feel humiliated if our irrational thinking is exposed. We even learn to manipulate another in order to gain a scrap of reassurance. We scan for a raised eyebrow or a tense voice when describing sensations and symptoms. However, this is another outer chasing that will not heal health anxiety. A healthier reassurance is found in knowing 1) that consuming the powerful immune fortification of plants will give health protection and wellbeing and 2) that you are now competent to handle health needs and/or anxiety appropriately (Wehrenberg 2008). Rule in Recovery: allowing oneself reassurance one time only helps stop the broken record and roller coaster fear waves from ruminating and intruding continuously. Just for today.

4. Those with health anxiety check the body repeatedly, taking magnifying glasses to their body or palpating tissue to the point of soreness and redness. This checking can become obsessive to the point of an

Chapter Three: Mind Care

illusionary reality: "Wait! Did I see some blood or didn't I? Wait! Did I see an enlargement or didn't I? Maybe I did! Get the flashlight!" It is not helpful to constantly check the body. The body has little aches, pains, and changes over the course of every day. Hypervigilance towards every sensation provides little useful information and fuels catastrophic thinking. Do not check and recheck or scan for a problem even though the insistent push to scan is strong. The truth is you will notice a real problem, and you will not go back to scan, inadvertently making an imagined problem worse. Don't cave into that first catastrophic scan. Instead assert: "I am practicing healing tools of new thinking, plant nourishment, and intuition!" They are part of true immunity and protection from a "What if?" hell. When safety behaviors are deliberately avoided for a few hours or a few days, anxiety levels decrease. Make a commitment that just for today, you will not check your body, medical sites, or speak with other people about your concerns. Just for today.

When anxious, the amygdala hijacks the frontal lobe like a wild horse galloping out of control with the rider helplessly unable to stop the furious pace. Even though the amygdala does not lose its fear reactivity easily, we can train and give this horse peace. Unstopped, these defensive safety behaviors continue and prolong health anxiety because rational thinking is not practiced and intuition is not accessed.

Thinking That Stinks

Anxiety disorders involve disaster thoughts that repeatedly travel nerve pathways becoming ruts of negativity. Hence, the imperative need to stop the catastrophic and unrealistic thoughts from deteriorating into the negative domino effect of hours, days, or even weeks of destructive rumination towards that sensation or observation. Like I did with my birthmark.

The more that anxiety runs rampant, the more anxiety grows and facilitates learned helplessness.

Most people have some degree of a thinking bias that influences or distorts reality processing for overly optimistic, chronically pessimistic, or neutral outcomes. Seeing life through a chronically pessimistic lens is referred to as 'stinkin' thinking.' If you've got an anxiety disorder, then you've got at least one stinkin' thinking error, which when combined with safety behaviors can heighten the sense that one's health is threatened. Ruminating on these intrusive, catastrophic thoughts increases their frequency and intensity and the sense that the problem is truly bad. The more that anxiety runs rampant, the more anxiety grows and facilitates learned helplessness. Repetitive alarm triggering makes the amygdala more primed for threats that stimulates the stress response that further triggers the amygdala. A highly sensitized amygdala with implicit painful memories can lead to ongoing anxiety that no longer has anything to do with present circumstances. However, trying to control or deny crazy thinking is like trying to stop a gushing hose by putting your hand over the roaring leak. Let's look at these thinking errors and regain healthy, reasonable thinking by helping the mind-body to stay calm.

Thinking errors may include:

1. All-or-nothing thinking: I am either completely healthy or I am ill. Therefore, I need to frequently monitor my body to be certain of my health at all times.

2. Over-generalizing and overestimating negativity: using limited evidence to hold a belief, such as when hearing a bad health story that has similarities to my age and gender, and magically thinking the same will happen to me.

3. Discounting the positive with mental filtering/selective attention: focusing on the evidence supporting worrisome thoughts and overlooking the positive. If measures of good health are present, they must be some fluke and don't count. Ask yourself what does count then. Stop yourself from saying, "Even though I take care of myself with diet, exercise, and stress management, I am still a magnet for illness."

4. Catastrophizing: jumping from any questionable sensation to deadliness. "What if? It probably is!" Panic sweeps over you. This is a chance to really acknowledge the dramatic and crazed leap of catastrophic thinking.

5. Emotional reasoning: believing something to be true because it feels true. But where is the feeling coming from? Is it from anxious impulses or the wisdom of intuition? The imagination of an anxiety disorder is strong and convincing. "There must truly be

Chapter Three: Mind Care

something wrong otherwise I wouldn't feel so anxious." Well, no. This deduction is another crazed leap in thinking.

6. Personalization: taking events personally. "It is my fault that I have this condition or have health anxiety. I should feel good and have control over my health all the time."
7. Superstitious/magical worry: "If I think I am well, then I will tempt fate. If I don't worry about this, the worst may happen, so worry I must." Or talking about disease can make it happen. "I need to worry to mitigate my shame, show my compassion for others who suffer, and/or protect my health." There is also concern if a new illness is discovered, then this increases the likelihood of contracting that illness.
8. Fortune telling and mind reading: "The doctor didn't look me in the eye, so he secretly knows something is wrong and won't tell me."
9. Labeling: rating myself as defective: "I am fragile, volatile, intellectually handicapped, a magnet for (health) disaster. I will never be free of fear and worrying." No one is 100 percent healthy all the time. We all have grades of fluctuating health states varying throughout the day, week, month, and year.

Dysfunctional thoughts are like bullies coming at you, finding your weak link and rampaging your mind. Labeling dysfunctional thoughts strengthens this link and orders these little bullies to back off. You can even thank your mind for its contribution. "I am having an intrusive thought that because my heart skipped a beat and then thumped, this means I might be having a heart attack. Thank you for wanting to protect me, but my stable, calm brain recognizes this catastrophic thinking error, and I know I am fine." Correcting thinking errors empowers your frontal lobe to stay in charge and think from a sound mind.

Let's back up a little and note that in order to dismantle these thinking distortions, one must have the desire to heal completely. Any lurking secondary gain of worrying must be banished. Secondary gains of worrying about health include: anxiety providing a distraction from another challenge in life, staying a victim, gaining attention, and believing worry will protect one from illness and stave off death. If these secondary gains are not rooted out, it will be very difficult or even impossible to release worrying. Write an inventory on any secondary gains you may have. A common secondary gain is the belief that worry purges you of shame and guilt. It does not. Notice the shame and guilt keep coming back anyway? Secondary gain may also contain the belief that shame and guilt ironically protects you from illness. How wrong is that? Worrying depresses the immune system. Staying a victim is oppressive and burdensome for you and others who find they feel pity towards you. What helps you to live a long, happy life is a healthy lifestyle, not worry. Writing down these false gains shines a light on them, giving insight and motivation to release them.

> *In order to dismantle these thinking distortions, one must have the desire to heal completely.*

Here are some limbic-dominated reactions that are negatively reactive and somewhat hysterical during an inner dialogue:

- "He's no good!" versus "We have different perspectives regarding this issue, and I'm really irritated with him right now. But I am learning to accept in him what is unlikely to change."

- "I'm no good!" versus "I am slowly getting this sewing skill. I am frustrated to the point of wanting to throw a bomb into this sewing room, but I won't. I will ask for help instead."

- "My body is no good!" versus "I am feeling or seeing something strange right now. My reactive body has a habit of doing that."

- "Everything is a disaster! My house, car, and clothes are ruined! Will my dog ever smell dog-like again? The Internet said a skunked dog will stink for two years!" versus "This stinks that my dog was sprayed by a skunk, but I won't believe everything I read or hear. I will apply this be-gone skunk remedy and solve this problem."

Belief intensifies sensations, which leads to thinking that interferes with taking control. This dysfunction may be viewed in the following dialogue:

Chapter Three: Mind Care

The amygdala states, "I am so tired. Why? Could I have a brain tumor? What if? No!" This message is sent to cortex. The PFC makes a decision to stop catastrophizing and be realistic about sensations and observations.

The pre-frontal cortex says, "Oh, that's right, my adrenals are overwhelmed. I am OK!"

After researching, an adrenal health relief message floods the brain. It is calm for a moment, but then the amygdala screams out, "But maybe this time it really is an early brain tumor, and I do not even know it!"

The pre-frontal cortex jumps back in, "Stop it now! Please!" But fear now races ahead, leaving the PFC in the dust.

There has got to be a better way to think.

Thinking That is Sweet

Well, there is. Let's go back to square one and ask: do I actually have the illness or the fear of having the illness? These are two very different things. The problem is with worry, not health. Does worry really protect me from becoming ill? No. Worrying is the devil's prayer. Worrying leads to anxiety and misery, and along with being unrealistic and a waste of time, it hurts nearly every aspect of living. We need to treat health anxiety as a worry problem and not a health problem.

Observe how anxiety leaps to lay its claim on your mind and how much mileage it gets from some sensation or from stories of others who contracted some dreadful thing. For example, some can panic when a rough stool scratches the lower rectum, creating a little blood streak. "Oh no, the guy down the street just died from colon cancer!" This innocent little blood gives a big mileage jolt for the anxiety pathway when it is actually nothing. Do not believe everything your anxious mind tells you. Marianne Williamson wrote, "You must master a new way of thinking before you can master a new way to be." Know that thoughts can run your life, and what thoughts you allow are what thoughts continue. So let's break up the train of thinking errors and have a new mind.

The brain is habitual and does what it is used to doing for better or for worse. Any negative thought that is repeated more than once initiates a nerve pathway rut that when established takes time and effort to extinguish. But the brain also wants to be challenged with learning something new and solving a mystery. Believe you me, the brain wants to be free of anxiety, which hurts it, your mind, and your soul. The choice to use the executive decision maker, the left PFC, to re-route this thinking error rut and override the emotional dominance of the limbic system leaves behind dysfunctional thoughts while embracing a new way to think.

To tap into the chief brain executive and assess what its critical and rational thinking skills say apart from the hysterics of the anxiety threat-based circuit, stop and ask: "Rational mind, what do you think about this strange gut cramp?" Stop and listen for the answer, even say the answer out loud: "I have felt this kind of cramp before, and it is not worth worrying about." Stay in the moment versus the mind projecting fatality just around the bend. You can also count from one to ten to give time for the frontal lobe to think versus reacting and also waiting fifteen minutes before performing a compulsion, which is the amount of time it takes to overcome any dysfunctional craving. Simultaneously, breathe slowly and deeply while you focus on the message from your rational mind. Deep breathing opens up a tight chest and a tightly coiled anxious mind. It helps you identify the trigger-response pattern and stand up to it. The rational mind detaches from being taken down by anxiety's dire agitation yet again, and it increases PFC strength and its neural network of rational thinking.

Fear escalates when we give into it; giving control over to destructive anxiety is debilitating.

Face the fear, and it will shrink and turn from you. Stop feeding the fear, and it will fade. F.E.A.R. = Face Everything And Recover. This is also known as extinguishing the anxiety through systematic desensitization, a behavioral technique to treat anxiety and phobias. To desensitize anxiety, first write out an anxiety hierarchy beginning from mild anxiety provoking experiences to more intense situations such as reading about a disease to receiving a diagnostic test. Then, release all tension using muscle relaxation, breathing, or meditating (fear is not compatible with relaxation), as you expose yourself to each level of the hierarchy slowly but surely. Many of us who have struggled with health anxiety also have a death phobia. How do you apply graded exposure to a death phobia? Try to have a near-death experience or go into a coma? Well, no. Maybe being with someone who is dying and feels great peace or reading about others who have had near-death experiences would help.

Recognizing the fact that disease does exist, and it does hurt and even kill others is a good first step. Breathe. Stay. Go onto the next level where disease is further verified by hearing someone speak of having an illness or that someone died of that illness, maybe even someone of your age and gender. Breathe. Stay. Spend time in a hospital filled with ill patients and breathe through that, too. The belief that this information and experience will make the disease more likely to fly into our lives is a superstition.

Chapter Three: Mind Care

How rational is a superstition? Take each superstition-filled thought and start breathing through it, and then go onto the next level of fear while you practice rational thinking: "I am calm and protected by plants.... I am calm and protected by something stronger than this anxiety...."

Cognitive reframing is a crucial tool that allows one to leap away from thinking errors and resume appropriate thinking within the reasonable frontal lobe. Even though the habit brain is reflexive and faster than the rational cortex, cognitive reframing retrains the brain to depend upon rational thinking instead of knee-jerk thinking. The remedy begins with the recognition of habitual, distorted thinking. When a reflexive thinking error goes off, such as, "There is something seriously wrong with my throat! It has felt parched for three days now," rate the stress level of anxiety from one to five (with five being the most intense anxiety) and identify the thinking error: "There goes (catastrophic, superstitious, emotional reasoning, etc.) thinking again. Strong, but just a thinking error." With these steps, a space is created between you and the distorted thought, allowing the PFC to step in and take control of the distortion. This fosters a healthy relationship with your thoughts and less succumbing to the alarm impulse.

Hogan and Young write of the importance of disputing the alarm impulse: "What evidence do I have to support or not support this thought? What is the probability of this being a disaster?" Ask yourself whether these thoughts are fair and realistic. Could this sensation be related to something else besides illness? "Am I overestimating the risk? What is a less extreme way of looking at this sensation? The truth is that it is more likely to be innocent than bad. What would I tell a friend who had this worry?" Focus on a sensible thought and replace the thought distortion with a reasonable non-catastrophic option such as, "I have been overly using my voice; I have eaten too much salty food; the medication I have been taking is very drying; I have not been drinking enough water." After grasping the sensible thought while breathing out the tension, re-rate anxiety from one to five again. Even if the number has only decreased by half, anxiety is now in the process of being tamed.

Here are two tools that also work to sharpen differentiation between rational and irrational thinking (Hogan and Young 2007): a pie chart can be drawn with each cause of a sensation representing a slice of the pie. For example, if you have a headache, each pie slice is given a possible cause of the headache such as muscle tension, hormonal and normal physical fluctuations, too much fat and offensive foods, sinus congestion, excess toxins in circulation, or lack of sleep. Put your greatest fear of what's causing the headache on one slice of the pie. Rate each one from one to ten in likelihood of that being the cause of the headache (Hogan and Young 2007). This helps to restore rational thinking as one begins to see that it is significantly less likely that a sensation has been caused by something bad.

With catastrophic thinking, we must ask what evidence do we have to jump to this conclusion? "I notice that I am having that thought and telling myself a negative story again." That perceived awfulness ignores the low likelihood of illness and blindly focuses on the distorted interpretation. The catastrophic option shrinks to a very small percentage. On my pie chart, there is a large slice for a reactive mind and body. It also includes one for adrenal fatigue, dumping toxins, carrying a higher acidic load, and normal daily variations. Another helpful tool is designing a pyramid of how many people who might be experiencing this same sensation as you would have it checked, how many would need further investigation, how many would have a serious disorder requiring strong medicine or surgery, and how many would be untreatable? Two out of one hundred at the top of the pyramid might be untreatable. The odds are in your favor.

A problem solving principal during medieval times and that is still used today is Occam's Razor: the simplest explanation for any question or finding is usually the most accurate explanation. Too many "ifs" is a sign of too much complexity. Investigate the simplest theory first. In recovery from health anxiety, we look for probable explanations of bodily manifestations, not certainty. Thoroughly examine the evidence to identify the basis of our distorted thoughts. Rule in recovery: keep it simple. I mean, why shouldn't a mole itch? It is skin, too. Why shouldn't one have explosive stools here and there? The hardworking intestines have a right to rebel and get rid of toxins and irritants. When taking care of yourself, think of the odds not the stakes. Truthfully, the chance of something bad happening is very small. Almost all people who are taking care of themselves are not living with a serious illness today. Serious illness amidst a healthy lifestyle is the extreme exception. Keep it simple.

Fight back against distorted and anxious thinking. Although somatic manifestations can be sudden and uncomfortable, they do not mean that one is definitely and imminently ill. A fire alarm is ringing, but there is no fire. Healthy, sweet thinking discerns the lack of fire from the alarm going off: "Loud alarm going off. I've heard, felt, or seen this before. I deserve to stand up to this fireless alarm and with all my courage, I will!" Even if you feel no courage, stand up anyway to this false alarm. Fake it till you make it. Just fake it because if one stays in fight-or-flight for too long, this can lead to panic, headaches, and stomach distress. How helpful is that?

Give yourself a chance to think fairly and realistically. Thinking errors must be refuted over and over again with strong effort. Remember that these thinking errors have been cultivated for a long time—years, usually—and that it will take time to dismantle them. Give yourself sixty to ninety days to change this negative habit and create a new one. Each day repeat affirmations such as, "An angel of health is walking with me. I am protected by the healing power of plants infused by the sun. I am free of irrational fears about my health." Continue to repeat these affirmations to move away from a well-entrenched negative thought rut. Yes, there is short-term vulnerability and awkwardness in the beginning of recovery, as you let go of a very familiar way of thinking, but this is the breakaway pain for the long-term gain of recovery. The more balanced feelings that result will be worth the struggle. When you continue to identify, dispute, and alter these irrational thoughts, it becomes natural and even ingrained like driving a manual shift car and no longer having to concentrate on shifting gears.

Cognitive-behavioral therapy works to change destructive thinking into realistic, rational thinking that leads to brain control and peace. Many people have healed from health anxiety, and you are no exception to this victory. You're up.

Obsessive Disorder

Health anxiety has an obsessive quality to it and can overlap with the somatic axis in obsessive-compulsive disorder (OCD). OCD is a neurological impairment involving intrusive, unwanted, unreasonable, and in this case "What if?" thoughts and fears that intrude mercilessly in a cyclical and repetitive manner. OCD involves a biochemical imbalance, i.e. reduced serotonin activity in the PFC and increased dopamine activity in the basal ganglia, which results in a malfunctioning of the brain's thinking gearshift. Efforts to control these obsessive thoughts and relieve the obsessive distress with compulsive rituals, such as repetitive hand washing, is futile. It is the obsessive doubting, not ubiquitous germs, that is the main problem. Although both health anxiety and OCD can involve compulsive checking, thinking errors, and intolerance for uncertainty, health anxiety fears center around having an illness while obsessive-compulsive disorder is marked by intrusive thoughts and fears of contamination and contracting an illness or transmitting an illness to another. OCD is no longer classified as an anxiety disorder and has been placed under Obsessive-Compulsive and Related Disorders. Obsessive-OCD or "pure-O" occurs without debilitating compulsive behaviors attempting to undo anxiety such as washing hands, walls, or even a street a hundred times a day. The degree, type, frequency, and severity of OCD manifestations vary from person to person.

Health obsessions revolve around themes that include contamination, somatic and uncertainty subtypes of which a person may have more than one subtype. Within the uncertainty subtype lies pathological doubting (about health) and an intolerance for (health) uncertainty. Usually an irresistible compulsion to perform rituals that "undo" the anxiety as repeatedly washing hands or walls or seeking reassurance that the health worry is unfounded follow the intrusive image. Contamination obsessions involve fear of dirt, germs, bodily fluids, contracting a disease, being poisoned or contaminating another person. The somatic subtype includes concern with illness and/or part of the body, or other body related obsessions.

Internet health and disease researching, seeking reassurance, body checking, or excessive washing and grooming can become a time consuming compulsion that feeds the health obsession and does not resolve the obsessive distress attacks. While some may not think anything is out of the ordinary, many with obsessive compulsive disorder have intrusive and disturbing thoughts they know are bizarre, yet they can't shake them off without performing a ritual to calm the limbic system, even if just for a moment. Relief may arrive, but then another piece of information comes along, creating fresh fear so the amygdala screams once again, "I can have signs and symptoms of this disease and not even know it!" Cycle repeats.

How does this work? According to Jeffrey Schwartz, MD, who wrote *Brain Lock*, the putamen (a round structure as the base of the forebrain, which is the front part of the brain, including the cerebral hemispheres, thalamus and hypothalamus) is the automatic transmission for moving the body while the caudate nucleus helps shift the brain into balanced and realistic thinking. With OCD, the fear circuit becomes hyper-metabolic and gets stuck in gear, as an alarm impulse travels from the amygdala to the orbitofrontal cortex (OFC), the error detection circuit, and keeps firing inappropriately from lack of proper filtering from the caudate. Because thinking gears are not shifting properly, the overactive caudates repeatedly tell the OFC that something is not right and something needs to be done about it. The cingulate gyrus, which is wired to the heart and gut, produces the sinking stomach feeling that something terrible will happen if you don't check (with the doctor, a journal, or the Internet) and check again. Reality testing of irrational fear becomes weak, and anxious

Chapter Three: Mind Care

thoughts are stuck and continue to spin in our minds. The fear circuit locks with continual bombardment of disturbing thoughts, and life is experienced as a large and repetitive fear magnet. For example, if my finger is twitching, I immediately fear that I have amyotrophic lateral sclerosis or a brain tumor. Whoa! The reality is a twitching finger only rarely means those two possibilities and is much more commonly associated with simple nerve irritation.

Dogs can suffer from OCD as well. Their OCD is connected to brain circuitry and chemistry malfunctioning. According to Susan Klavon in *The Whole Dog Journal*, common canine OCD behaviors include tail chasing, fly snapping, light chasing, and licking. Hallucinations may be present, which can cause the dog to chase things that are not there. The prevalence is around 1 percent to 8 percent of dogs, beginning as young as three months of age and is thought to be due to a genetic defect. As in humans, untreated OCD commonly progresses in dogs needing lifelong care with possible medication (i.e. antidepressants and anticonvulsants), self-calming skills, and behavioral management with plenty of exercise as an energy outlet. I would add that placing the dog on a largely plant-based diet (dogs can thrive as vegetarians and live longer without eating meat or dairy products) along with these interventions will give healing for canine OCD.

Healing begins when one can assert these images are nothing more than intrusive thoughts of health dysfunctions coming from a locked mental gearshift. See the anxiety as an electrical current passing through your mind and body. Like health anxiety, recovery from OCD is an ongoing task that usually subsides in frequency with the practice of claiming these impulses for what they are. Sometimes exaggerating the fears can shrink them: "This freckle will explode in three days, I just know it!" A realigned mental transmission system can override the fear loop. The highest thinking part of the brain—the PFC—needs to identify the thinking error and take over the shifting function in order to restore balanced thinking and thwart excess activity in the fear circuit. Claim and come to know "there goes this disorder again." This averts identifying and submerging into the false message of irrational fear and frees you from its snare.

This new role of the PFC, along with facing the feared situation and resisting all rituals, builds tolerance for uncertainty. Along with soothing words and phrases, affirmations (as in "peace, truth, God, strength, I am safe"), and claiming the powerfully protective lifestyle that you live by works to change brain chemistry. Despite the challenge of health anxiety, being within the realm of possibility more so than other distressful images of striking a loved one or screaming blasphemies in church, one can shift over to the PFC and respond, "This is not me, it's OCD" or " I have obsessive thoughts, but I am not those thoughts" or "Oh, this is my brain giving me an erroneous message again. There you go again with a catastrophic or all-or-nothing or magical thought. No! Healthy brain is in charge now!" These responses allow you to break out of the groove that the obsession has established for itself. Acceptance of having an anxiety disorder ironically weakens an attack, so surrender to win! The PFC is completely capable of embracing being in charge and claiming victory!

There is no easier, softer way. Catastrophic, ruminative fears and compulsions to perform safety behaviors are intrusive and can occur hundreds of times a day. Immediately call them for what they are just as many times back. Then distract yourself with something that is positive: sewing, yard work, dancing with music, being with friendly and fun two-legged and four-legged loved ones, doing whatever you love to do that is good for your soul. Excessively staring into a TV, cell phone, or tablet does not strengthen one's soul and instead promotes zombiness. Use these screens for their wealth of information and then get out. Prevent boredom, as obsessions will look to fill empty mental and physical space. Practice affirming that the obsessive catastrophic fear-thought is a symptom of health anxiety. Remind yourself that this anxiety is due to a chemical imbalance, along with an enlarged and sensitive amygdala and a stuck anterior cingulated gyrus (ACG). Practice this even when immersed in the fear, and you don't feel like it. Sometimes having courage, standing up for yourself, and taking that leap of faith is required to embrace the great probability of a sensation being harmless.

Sometimes having courage, standing up for yourself, and taking that leap of faith is required to embrace the great probability of a sensation being harmless.

STOP!

A thought comes in. It is either positive, negative, or neutral. Non-neutral thinking evokes feelings, and feelings are louder and faster than

Chapter Three: Mind Care

thoughts. So, while we may feel powerless over our intrusive thoughts and feelings, it is possible to unravel this powerlessness when we recognize our lack of reasonable thinking when anxiety hits. Cognitive blocks begin with "Oh no, I can't, I won't, I'm finished, what if, this is awful." This "awfulizing" sways thinking in a continued negative manner. What good is it? As soon as this kind of knee-jerk thinking begins, assert "STOP!" and practice rational thinking with relaxed breathing—just for this moment. Stop negative and nonsensical thinking before it can take hold of and perpetuate a paralyzed victim stance. It is essential to recognize and interrupt the broken record of anxiety before it gains momentum as negative health thoughts act as kindling for an anxiety bonfire. When you realize that a thought is uselessly negative, immediately see a large red stop sign or someone slicing the air yelling "NO! STOP!" You can even yell out, "NO! STOP!" Then switch to a positive thought: a beautiful place, a person or animal you love, God taking care of you, or a project you are working on and love. If practiced over and over, a new brain pathway will be created, as neurons make new connections with one another to create new thinking habits. We can learn to use our brain to change our brain.

We can learn to use our brain to change our brain.

Health anxiety greatly behooves one to live and focus in the present moment. Am I good now? Anxiety is always future disaster oriented. I am good now. Rule in recovery: no obsessing about the future. One woman who feared a future return of rogue cell clumping (I just don't like the word cancer. Or malignancy or biopsy. Even the word tumor is pushing it. I like the word rogue, as though cancerous cells are just pesky pirates to throw off of your ship) practiced thought stopping 100 times a day. Her catastrophic thinking dwindled and receded, freeing her from the need to thought stop so frequently. A highly sensitive amygdala is not easily tamed, and initially, you may also need to practice thought stopping 100 times a day. Oh, so what; you are worth that hard work.

We need predictability to maintain a realistic perspective. Loss of perspective creates suffering: "Something bad will happen; I am not safe." Thought management intercepts the fear loop from going round and round, as though you are caught in a dryer. Identify catastrophic thinking and ask, "Am I immediately imagining a worst-case scenario?" If yes, then yell silently or out loud "STOP!" Is my life health based? If yes, then yell "STOP!" again. And then state: "This kind of anxious thought is coming from my anxiety disorder. I won't trust this thought; it's a form of hysteria." The goal of thought stopping is to eliminate arousal of ruminative anxiety and keep the anxious mind cool. Thought stopping and thought replacement create a new positive neuro-pathway: "Self! Stop it! I am nourished and protected by sun-infused plants that give true healing! God's healing light of intuition is shining in me now!" Smash it! "STOP! I recognize this catastrophic thought, and if I detach from it, it will fade, and I will triumph over it! I will rise above these broken brain gears and be triumphant!" In recognizing these mental messages as false, I remain in the present moment. I am learning to contain the worry and get distance from it. I am able to recognize an obsessive thought as only a thought with a distinctive breathless feeling to it. I begin to control my reaction to these types of thoughts versus diving into them. I further know that they are the result of a chemical imbalance and well-traveled rut in my brain.

Dr. Margaret Wehrenberg asks in *The Ten Best-Ever Anxiety Management Techniques*, was a feeling of dread or nervousness present before the scary thought? Yes? Then that scary thought is even more likely to be random mental trash. Dread can come out of nowhere thanks to an unregulated autonomic nervous system, and it frequently means nothing. This dread feeling could also be the result of low blood sugar, a food sensitivity, or high histamine levels, etc. An excess of norepinephrine and inadequate serotonin will stimulate the autonomic nervous system, leading to an uneasy gut sensation and fragile doom feeling. A problem can always be found and exaggerated. The PFC can step in, quickly analyze and assert: "This is a random surge of stress hormones stimulating my autonomic system. I don't have to fall prey to this. In fact, I won't."

People struggling with health anxiety have vivid imaginations. A questionable sensation occurs and a bad movie starts with you as the bamboozled star. From now on, when the bad movie starts, yell "STOP!" Then visualize kicking some serious butt and seeing that this time you are the hero of this movie. Strange drama-infested sensation? Cut! "I will not fail to notice a real problem. If a real problem were to happen, I will handle it with my box of healing tools." Make it easier for serotonin to help the PFC stay in charge and slow the overactive limbic system, thwarting the rumination of the cingulate gyrus. It is common to believe: "If I have this feeling (that nags me into the ground), there must be a reason for it (further nagging me into the ground)." Boom! Back to the fear waves! Cognitive distortion has yet again come to pay a not-so-friendly call to create anxiety like a (scary looking) clown pumping up fear balloons. If I am having a rumination (that maybe I have even had before), there must be some truth to it, yes? Well, no. If I have a rumination it is just that, a rumination, and needs to be blown up out of the water.

Plan!

The ambiguity of a potential problem is less tolerable for anxiety prone people. The haze of maybe yes, what if, maybe no, is just too much. But here is the guide from Dr. Wehrenberg to follow from now on: if you can't identify a specific problem that can be solved, then it is merely worry, not a real problem. Positive thought replacement is therefore sufficient. Ask: is this a true problem or worry? If it is a real problem, make a plan that helps contain the anxiety.

If I twisted my ankle and cannot put any weight on it, I will get an x-ray to see if I broke anything. Resolve "What if?" ruminating with action plans. "Stop! I have a plan!' and thought replace. A health worry is most often simply a worry to process, not an actual illness. A plan helps the ACG get unstuck and creates an opportunity for the amygdala to observe how this situation turned out OK, just like the last time the same hyped-up alarm thoughts happened. A clear plan of action is soothing to the amygdala. If a worry (unspecific potential problem) occurs that obviously can't be solved right now, stop and replace your thoughts with images of gaining victory over this disorder and what you will be doing in five years. Tell yourself that plants have the sun's energy within them and are now healing your body right and left! You have the strength of your left brain, you have a plan, and you have already worried, so forget about it. The one second rule is that one can think of the fear thought for only one second to keep that thought from getting a foot hold in the circuitry. Don't let it go round and round again.

Triggers found in media, stories, memories, life experiences, and/or nervous system blips provoke health worries for almost everyone and not just for we health anxietians. Rule in recovery: recognize that these triggers offer an opportunity to practice the challenge of overcoming them and thereby weaken the progression of this disorder. When the trigger comes, exclaim, "I will now practice standing up to this anxiety!" We become more resilient towards health doubts, and they simmer down. Effort must be used from the frontal boss brain to manage dysfunctional deeper structures. Darren Sims, who wrote *Conquering Health Anxiety*, speaks of being ready with a relapse prevention plan. For instance, write this down on flash cards and have this reaction ready: "The next time I feel or think of something that creates anxiety, I will not fall for this thought and fear. Instead, I will jump up and down and shout, 'I am fine! I am fine! I am fine!'" I will practice slow breathing and calming self-talk for thought and feeling management. It may take months before the anxious mind is tamed. One may notice that the anxiety initially gets worse upon thought stopping and replacement. Yet, keep on! Anxiety will revolt and dig in harder, as it will be threatened of ending its livelihood of exerting its vampire-like existence upon your energy. Well, I'm sorry, anxiety, but you have been a bad tick, and I must extract you now, so goodbye.

I Will Not Fail

Because anxiety results in over interpreting sensations, helpful thoughts that would balance thinking and keep it reasonable can be missed. For example, the lip thing again: "This peeling and burning lip again! Is it lip malignancy?? No!" Breathe. Wait. "Oh, that's right, that lip balm I used has lemon oil in it, and that's what is irritating my lip." Anxiety makes us forget to breathe and pause. It also obscures the capacity to differentiate a worry from a true problem.

Have I ever failed to notice a real health problem? Every single health worry that I've ever had has never come true. I will not fail to notice a real problem, a true problem. A real problem beyond fibrocystic breasts, irritable bowel syndrome, migraine headaches (yes, they hurt unbearably, but they go away), and tongue blisters. Real trouble is not so elusive you have to go looking for it (Wehrenberg 2008). Most of what we worry about does not happen. A fear thought comes and needs to be diverted into "I will not fail to notice a true problem."

Because my brain and body are so bathed and fortified by thousands of phytonutrients, I have the clarity now to notice a true problem from a worry. Because I am so protected, I am safe. Even with a less than optimal lifestyle, many people live still until after eighty years old.

Health observations require a balanced approach of the two brains. The left-brain asserts, "I have a nice little memory bank, and I will not fail to notice something important" while it assesses and differentiates sensory stimuli. The right brain intuits with a trust in something higher: "Because of this wave of truth that just went through me, I now deeply know I am OK and that this fear thought is bunk." I know I can wait for guidance and deeper knowing versus the knee-jerk reaction of catastrophic thinking.

Chapter Three: Mind Care 93

Remember the truth: I am protected by plants (that are not made by human hands) that fortify my highly sensitive nervous system. I accept normal health risk without freaking out just like I do when crossing the street. I can control my reaction to an irrational thought rather than fighting the thought itself, which only intensifies the thought. It is essential to believe that I am capable of differentiating rational from irrational thoughts. I will not be dragged under by ruminative thinking that promotes an off-the-wall scenario. My intuition is always here, and I will not fail.

Evaluate—See?

There are times when we feel lucid and become seized by the now recognized overreaction and irrational alarm of health anxiety: "What? I felt afraid of a simple canker sore? That is ridiculous." This jolt of reality testing helps to tame and teach the amygdala that another false alarm has gone off again. This sensitive and hyperreactive amygdala that warns us of (not) dangerous sensations is thankfully able to unlearn irrational fear, and therefore, it is able to desensitize trauma that is not really trauma. So, let's go. Let's give assistance to our amygdala to rein in catastrophic thinking and restore rational thinking.

After another attack of anxiety debauchery that proves to be false yet again, ask yourself what made the anxiety quiet down. Was it a piece of knowledge or an intuitive rush of peace? Was it remembering that this is just another anxiety flare that is just a part of having an anxiety disorder? Being with people who are not anxious? The passage of time and distraction? This identification of what was calming teaches the amygdala that some things don't need to be scary. And, in turn, it strengthens the PFC to keep fearful thoughts from going down the fear circuit. Victory!

Here is an example: during a meal you suddenly feel a pain in the middle of your chest as you swallow. No other symptoms. You feel the food slowly going down your esophagus and getting stuck with an intense sharp pain. Instead of freaking out, your left brain says, "Esophageal spasm," and your right brain says, "I am OK. Something is irritating my gullet. What am I eating? A hard-boiled egg? A dry piece of fish? These awful foods, no more!" Continuing to evaluate the outcome of another fear attack helps the pre-frontal cortex, anterior cingulate gyrus, and orbital-frontal cortex to take note and relay this good news to the basal ganglia, which can brainstorm anti-anxiety tactics and strengthen motivation to beat out these thoughts. You can then tell your amygdala: "ya see?" Focusing on the positive outcome reinforces the desensitization of fear and teaches the amygdala to be less reactive and afraid of alarms that you know are false. If the amygdala could speak, it would say, "Yes, I would like to be less reactive and afraid. Self, thank you for helping me."

Lucid Living

During sleep the content of dreams reflect one's physical and mental condition and also reveals one's truth, insight, warnings, and struggles. Dreaming of being lost in a large, decrepit city? Your mind needs to move from chaos, clutter, and dysfunctional thoughts into a new, clean, orderly mind. A spiritual mind. Mystical dreams, such as flying like a bird, reflect the potential passion and strength of one's spirit. Nightmares can make one jump out of sleep in a cold sweat, reflecting a toxic body and anguished soul. But here is the answer for these awful nightmares: instruct yourself before going to sleep to know you are dreaming when the bad dream appears. Resolve a nightmare by deciding to get in its face and defy it before you fall asleep. This is known as lucid dreaming. Practice the same technique with daytime anxiety. When you wake up in the morning, make a decision to get in anxiety's face when it strikes and defy it. The skill of lucid dreaming triumphs over these awful dreams when you realize you are dreaming and then get right in the persecutors face asserting, "You're only a dream! I can smash you!" The persecutor will shrink in the dream and in life! So much of the fear involved in an anxiety attack during waking hours is as fierce and false as the fear image within a bad dream. We may practice this same technique of lucid dreaming with lucid living by being ready to respond to the fear thought when it hits, saying, "You're only disordered anxiety! I will shrink you!"

A similar spiritual method can be done to heal difficult memories. We all have less than happy memories. Overwhelming experiences and memories can morph into post-traumatic stress disorder, which is when one deals with intrusive, traumatic memories that disrupt daily functioning with nightmarish reliving of the terrible scene. However, one can update these painful memories with re-scripting: take the memory and now see it with something that walked with and protected you, such as an angel or the Holy Spirit. Yes, there was terrible pain, but something got you through it. After all, you survived it. Once when I was five years old, a terrible thing happened. Something took me out of my body, and I floated safely up to the ceiling until it was safe to return to my body. That something is helping you now. No more feeling trapped as a victim of these past traumatic events.

Laughing

Have you ever noticed that being around laughing, non-anxious people distracts you from anxious preoccupation and helps you to regain perspective again? When someone laughs uproariously, those nearby cannot help but laugh, too; for you, this creates distance between you and a catastrophic thought. Laughter stimulates the vagus nerve and increases endorphins—the bliss and pain-no-more chemicals in our brains and bodies. It releases tension and activates the immune system, increasing natural killer cells. It gives the diaphragm an aerobic workout. Laughing enhances the communication between the two hemispheres of the brain and jolts the brain into a fun pathway, as it recirculates joy. So, let's laugh now! And let's laugh with our whole bodies instead of these stifled little head snorts and guffaws. Begin composing a laughing notebook filled with hilarious memories, comics, drawings, photographs, and anything else you find irrepressible and severely laughable. I have my own laughing book, and when I open that thing, it is not long before out of control laughing follows. Love it.

Certain people have elephant-like temperaments and are very calming. I love being around these elephants. A simple look from an elephant can knock the grip of irrationality away and resume clarity of thinking. Once when someone voiced anxiety about curved shaped stools, an elephant simply replied, "Yeah, the fear is crazy." Her rational calmness swept over him, and he felt free from the lunacy. For at least a moment.

The more clearly you see the hysteria of anxiety for what it is, which is only a distorted reaction, the more you will recognize its broken record pattern. "I'm terrified!" is replaced with "There goes that false terror thinking. I notice I am imagining the worst-case scenario, which is simply the anxiety disorder rearing up again. I don't have to fall into this nonsense." You are no longer as submerged and can separate, knowing it will fade away like after you wake up from a bad dream that seemed completely real. Anticipating anxiety before it strikes instead of feeling dismayed and shocked when it does strike lessens its interception of appropriate thinking. Each morning, one can acknowledge the possibility of anxiety visiting that day and to make the decision not to identify with its thinking error when it does visit. There is no reason to be swept away by its convictions. Add to this acknowledgement that you are powerless over your body's highly sensitive expressions, so when a strange sensation occurs, you will remember your body's nature and not be so easily terrified. This form of embracing anxiety ironically empowers you to stand up to this disorder. Instead of cowering to a catastrophic thought, we take that thought as a challenge to apply these skills and then rise above them. When anxiety strikes, it is an opportunity to put into action the tools of recovery. Yes, an opportunity! This is how you gut-wrenchingly make your recovery happen. Embrace the anxiety. Anxiety loses its power when you stand up to it.

> *Anxiety loses its power when you stand up to it.*

Make anxiety an object of laughter: the ridiculousness of each day being a musical chair of whatever somatic mayhem: today moles, tomorrow pelvic twitching, Wednesday throat raw and clamping, Thursday strange hives, Friday give me a break from this madness. So what if sensations and perceptions mysteriously move about or that anxiety levels fluctuate throughout an hour or a day? Anxiety, stress, and sensations all play upon each other, turning into an enlarging chaotic ball. The more negative thinking there is, the more negative thinking there will be. We are hyperaware of our bodies and tend to fixate on sensations. If a friend shows us a rash, we may feel like our skin is crawling. Even yawning is contagious. Everyone experiences uncomfortable sensations, but most ignore minor ailments and normal aggravations. Except we maniacs, the hypochondriacs. Just kidding.

Placebo and Nocebo

Double blind studies have shown that healing occurs when people have received a sugar pill, thinking it was a powerful breakthrough drug to cure an affliction from which they were suffering. The belief that a drug, plant, prayer, or fasting will heal an affliction and then does just that reveals the potent healing power of the mind. This mind-body phenomenon has been studied since at least 1950 and is known as the placebo response. One third of all medical healings are thought to result from the placebo response. It is actually quite miraculous despite being written off as insignificant. The placebo response involves endorphins that are deeply relaxing along with positive thoughts and emotions that can influence regulatory proteins that determine DNA expression. Every person may manifest the placebo response, including animals: blood pressure decreases,

Chapter Three: Mind Care

warts and ulcers disappear, colon inflammation decreases, cholesterol levels go down, swelling diminishes and terminal disease abates (Rankin 2013).

Negative and limiting beliefs can be instilled in children i.e. "this (whatever problem) runs in the family" etc. As children, how many of us were taught self-healing with plants and mental/spiritual fitness? Instead, we are taught to eat rottenly and then run to a doctor when there is a health concern, as though our bodies are none of our business. Our bodies and minds are our business, and we need to know that we have the potential to manifest infinite healing power of body and mind. Get rid of defaulted negativity and mental clutter to receive and manifest this healing power. What you give power to has power over you.

It is common for medical and nursing students to fear contracting the same diseases that they are studying, even showing similar symptoms to that disease. For example, multiple sclerosis has symptoms that are similar to the symptoms of stress experienced during school. You're sitting in a lecture hall listening to a now droning lecture while your head bobs "What is wrong with my neck?! My head is out of control!" Feeling fatigued from inadequate sleep and worrying about the upcoming exam, you stagger over to the drinking fountain. "What is wrong with my legs? Now I have to pee so badly; I am about to lose it! My vision is blurry from staring at the screen; my eyes aren't right! No! Wait! Something is wrong with me! Maybe I have multiple sclerosis!"

Negative beliefs can result in the "nocebo" effect that works when the mind contributes to illness, as when one is crushed with despair and has lost hope such as when you're told, "You have only six months left to live." Pronouncing this arbitrary time line ushers in death as a near certainty. This should be illegal. No disease is incurable. Cultures with hexing practices can usher in morbidity and death. In the same manner, superstitions, obsessions, anxieties, and negative beliefs can lead to a paralyzed victim stance, as anxiety gathers momentum in the fear pathway. But we do not have to become paralyzed.

Let's look at Norman Cousins, an American professor of medical humanities, political journalist, and world peace advocate. He laughed in the face of death and overcame illness, paralysis, and pain, living twenty-six more years after receiving a "few months left to live" death sentence. After a stressful trip to Russia during the post-cold war era that included adrenal exhaustion and hours of exposure to diesel fumes, he became ill and was diagnosed with ankylosing spondylitis, a degenerative collagen disorder causing constant pain and paralysis. Upon further research, it was thought that Cousins instead suffered from post-streptococcal reactive arthritis. Nevertheless, he obtained victory over a death sentence with uproariously hilarious laughter, watching comic films, receiving huge doses of intravenous vitamin C, stopping all medications, and ditching the hospital. Laughing very hard decreased his inflammatory markers and acted as an analgesic, giving him hours of pain-free sleep. He went on to write "Anatomy of an Illness" in 1979, describing this glorious healing, and concluded that a hospital is no place for a person who is seriously ill. We may share with Norman Cousins that laughter reflects the rapture of the human spirit and is our way back to health. It is our way back to maintaining magnificent health.

Health anxiety can be healed quickly or slowly. It is highly treatable, requiring practice and commitment to nourish and retrain the brain and spiritualize the mind. Even though we have a built-in negativity bias ultimately trying to protect us, we can stay in charge and practice planting flowers (strengthening the frontal lobe and intuition) instead of seeing nothing but weeds to pull (obsessing about negative possibilities). The coordination and harmony of the right brain along with left brain knowledge to problem solve rationally creates resilience towards mental illness, namely health anxiety. If either the left brain is strong enough to convince the right brain that there is no danger or the right brain is able to give the left brain its intuitive message that one is safe, one can be free. Yet the combination of reasonable thinking and intuition is the duo that will smash fear to bits.

Health anxiety can be healed quickly or slowly. It is highly treatable, requiring practice and commitment to nourish and retrain the brain and spiritualize the mind.

Chapter 4:
Spirit Care

Winston Churchill once said that if you are going through hell to keep going. Battling severe attacks of depression while being prime minister of England, he would know. So keep going until you land into the balm of spiritual health that springs from the deepest and richest part of the psyche, the part of us that is concerned with meaning, mystery, and love. Here, serenity and freedom from the snare of worthless and destructive anxiety is found. Abnormal anxiety is a reflection of spiritual distress needing spiritual treatment that takes healing to the deepest level; treatment attempts without care of the spirit will be superficial and short lived. Care of the spirit allows one to flourish and is our greatest healing tool. This is a power that goes beyond the ego, as the unleashed power within one's spirit gives people the energy to risk their lives for someone they love or something they believe in such as running into a burning house or fighting for one's country. Though we may harbor a deep habitual pessimism that is maintained by a hyperactive, hypersensitive, and enlarged amygdala, hijacking the frontal lobes and terrorizing the rest of the mind, spiritual fitness places wings on your back to send you into an illuminated awareness that recognizes and detaches from the mechanics of irrational anxiety.

Abnormal anxiety is a reflection of spiritual distress needing spiritual treatment that takes healing to the deepest level.

Beliefs of Self

The boundary between an honest character inventory and useless, destructive beliefs of self can merge together obscuring recognition of what needs to go and what needs to be worked on within oneself. Knowing that "math is not my strong point" versus brooding that "I'm so stupid" illustrates this difference. Maybe you will never become a calculus professor but to categorically conclude complete stupidity is another thinking error. Destructive self-beliefs, such as telling yourself, "I am worthless, a clumsy oaf, bad, a victim; when I die, I will dissolve into eternal oblivion," will entrap you and become your reality. Having health anxiety and calling yourself a hypochondriac casts implied shame and makes a greater impression if compounded by a difficult past. When shame is experienced frequently, "I'm so stupid; I can't believe this," one develops a pervading apprehension that the world is not safe or fun. Or if life feels safe and fun momentarily, we feel vulnerable and guarded, anticipating the other shoe to drop soon.

Ruthless self-attacks impair natural self-repair mechanisms, and it is almost impossible to tame the insatiable anxiety monster if one is bogged down with the coarseness of low self-esteem and self-hatred. To feel shame is to be human and non-sociopathic, but chronic and irrational shame is damaging to one's self-worth and erodes one's identity. Guilt is the feeling that I did something wrong; shame is the feeling that I am wrong. Insecure and doubtful self-worth impedes recovery along with superstition and psychic masochism. If I am self-critical, I have reason to allow bullying of myself by myself. A shame filled self-image weakens recovery efforts, giving fear leeway to run rampant. No one is without fault. Each of us deserves to be healthy and happy despite having inevitable flaws. Identify any core beliefs that hinder recovery such as believing one is inherently bad or inadequate and/or that the earth is too randomly filled with pain to have any hope. Yes, we have struggles and flaws, but does that mean I am a terrible savage? Yes, the world has had, does have, and will have overwhelming pain, but does that mean we give up and crawl under a rock?

Chapter 4: Spirit Care

How we respond to the harsh reality on Earth is ultimately our choice. Self-doubt and condemnation simply hold one back. Rule in recovery: believe in something precious within yourself and cling to this awareness. Visualize being free from irrational anxiety, and trust in the body's healing power. Try to do this every day, no matter how much the fear attempts to mow you down. Reflect on how you have made it this far. I mean, deeply reflect on this fact, and let it open a channel for healing power to flow. See health anxiety as far away and all your health blessings close to you.

Spiritual care demands rigorous honesty with one's self; we must face the good AND the less savory parts of ourselves. If I know myself, I will be a little savvier to anxiety's tricks and be less taken down by its whims. To deeply connect with something stronger than myself, I must not balk from seeing the totality of myself, as self-deception hinders hearing the still small voice of intuition, God's voice. While remaining rigorously honest, I can ask for help with my whole heart. Make a list of your strengths: your knowledge, your intuition, your self-care routine, your accomplishments, and your talents. What are your stumbling blocks and weaknesses? Do you have a hot temper, tend to procrastinate, or are prone to bouts of laziness? Just get them out on paper to be honest with yourself and obtain perspective. Focus on your strengths—most importantly that you exist, got up today, and that you sincerely want healing and are working to heal. Do whatever you have to do to love, care, and respect yourself. We need self-compassion and self-care, just as when we give a dear friend who is suffering. We need compassion for our thoughts that are still influenced by past negative experiences and still seen as facts; compassion for a biased memory and skewed thinking pattern that is nearly impervious to reason and healthy thinking; compassion for being vulnerable to fear and somatic sensitivities; and compassion for the struggle with obsession that is overwhelming at times and can take so much energy to transcend.

Our body is made stronger or weaker depending on our mental state. When that negative mental state is prolonged, the risk for illness is increased. And, if one ignores or is not aware of one's feelings or needs, the subconscious will find another way to signal the message that something is wrong with negative physical manifestations. Emotions can be health degrading such as shame, resentment, or apathy, which impair the immune system. Or emotions can be health enhancing such as love, laughter, optimism, empathy, acceptance, and joy that have a tonic effect on all organs. One gains the ability to identify and separate from pessimistic and limiting beliefs and thoughts, such as, "My worth is next to nothing" or "The world is not safe," and to process them as useless and harmful. Rule in recovery:

no self-condemnation. You must love yourself, as no amount of love from others is sufficient to fill the yearning for which your heart pleads.

Uncertainty

How do you feel about change? How much uncertainty can you tolerate? All of us are fallible, living in a toxic, uncertain, and yet beautiful world. The structures that are dysfunctional in an anxious brain are also sensitive to uncertainty. A sensation of uncertain origin may thrust one into an abyss of panic and desperation to feel safe. Trying to decipher its meaning becomes fruitless, groping into any available knowledge base of what, why, and how my body is doing what it is now doing. Regarding physiology and medical knowledge, we are conditioned to think that this sensation means that, and that the doctor is the ultimate expert of what our bodies are doing. Well, sometimes the doctor knows, and sometimes he or she does not know. More uncertainty. Will anyone ever master knowledge of the brain and body? There have even been studies trying to understand the physiology of itching. For those of us struggling with fear of illness and death, we may seek health certainty with safety behaviors that calm us temporarily but diminishes the ability to tolerate uncertainty in the long run. We may live a life of self-care to feel in control of our health yet still fall back into the vicious circle of health and fear obsession. Why? Because expecting something outside of ourselves, even if it is superbly capable of helping us, does not reach into the root of health anxiety. What is that root? Spiritual dysphoria. Much of the body is a mystery and will likely remain so. Part of being alive is acceptance of frailties and discomforts for what they are: random, sometimes bizarre, imperfections and baffling expressions that usually mean nothing. While we may face a level of unpredictability throughout our lives, it is important to recognize that a strong spirit is able to tolerate a large measure of uncertainty.

To move from this morass of uncertainty, let us begin to consider what may lie beyond our reality processing minds. Let us begin with something that is higher and more powerful than us: nature. Who would disagree with this? Think of brilliant starry skies when camping. The sun keeps the earth alive, and your loyal heart beats so tirelessly; these reflections are a practice in spiritual awareness. The overwhelming anecdotal evidence that the moon and weather can augment anxiety or heighten energy reflects a connection with nature and the universe. Many report waves of apprehension and bouts of insomnia just before and during a full moon, although this has been dismissed scientifically. Yet during a full moon, there are higher

Chapter 4: Spirit Care

levels of positive ions that drain and irritate people. Seasonal affective disorder occurs when there is less sunlight during autumn and winter months that can result in depression, irritability, and increased appetite and sleeping—bear-like behavior. Others may have the opposite of this seasonal disorder and feel agitated when the sun is at its brightest during summer afternoons. There is evidence that intense solar flares (sun storms) reach earth's atmosphere and affect its electromagnetic energy field as well as the electromagnetic field of humans to varying degrees. The pineal gland is affected by chaotic electromagnetic activity, resulting in a desynchronized circadian rhythm (Cherry 2002). During these times, one may experience heat or cold feet, heart palpitations, equilibrium imbalances, anxiety, irritability, lethargy, mood swings, chaotic thinking, nausea, headaches, insomnia, and tinnitus (Marshall 2014). Here is a chance to recognize dysfunctional, dysphoric thinking that may be more likely to occur during full moons, a tempestuous sun, and days with too much or too little light: "I feel like a lunatic from another planet. Why am I so drained for days now? Is something wrong with me?" into "This agitation. What are the sun and moon doing now? I guess I am resonating with them."

Moving from the concrete to the more abstract, how do you feel about spirituality? Indifferent, empty, wrought up, or disgusted with the thought of it? Know that fearful and cynical ideas about God activate the fear circuit and shortstops insight and farsightedness into the spiritual realm. "Fear is only inverted faith; it is faith in evil instead of good" (Florence Scovel Shinn). Remember that "God has not given us a spirit of fear, but of power and of love and of a sound mind" (2 Timothy 1:7 NKJV). Begin with what does have meaning for you. What is sacred to you? Is anything coming up? Can you resonate I AM deeply in your soul? Sort of, kind of, no? Well, there you go. Your soul is hungry. Silently and deeply within each one of us, minus psychopaths lacking a conscience, is a divine light of spiritual presence that longs to be held as sacred. This presence needs to be protected from various onslaughts to keep the light strong and clear. Habitual negative thinking and behavior are the worst of the onslaughts. Fight these tooth and nail. Can we call this divine light God? To feel I AM is to feel light, the light of God shining in your life. Start from where you are and ask your mind to open for a brief peep towards something that lies beyond, and feed your soul with this open-mindedness and other spiritual tools.

One thing that is certain is that our imperfect and limited egos need help to transcend the looming uncertainty of health anxiety. There is something higher than you or me that is running this life no matter what you do or do not believe. Is my life mine? Am I in charge of all this? Did I design my birth? Am I beating my own heart or propelling my intestines or exchanging carbon dioxide for oxygen in my lungs? Do I micromanage my inner ear to keep me from an unbalanced reality? You could quickly retort it's under the control of the autonomic nervous system, but what is running that? Do I know how long my life will be? Do I even want to know? Maybe my life isn't as much my life as I assume it is. So, am I in charge of all this? Maybe something else is ultimately. Science? Of course beautiful science is part of this mystery, and no one can deny that science ultimately enters the mystical realm where logic as we know it fades away. Think of subatomic particles that baffle logic by being in two places at the same time. But face it, Science, you need something higher as well to help unravel your mysteries and your uncertainty.

Spirituality runs on a continuum from non-religious mystical states to strong religious beliefs. Beliefs run from nihilism to structured constructs of a divine force or creator. From a neuroscientific perspective, research has shown a difference in spiritual and non-spiritual brains. Spiritual brains have been found to have thicker frontal lobes with more activity in this region. When non-believers were given dopamine, their brains began to appear more similar to the spiritual brains (Newburg 2012). Unbeknownst to atheists, they can suffer from spiritual distress, for we all need a sense of meaning in our lives. Atheists and agnostics are capable of having an awareness of something that enlightens but reject or question the existence of an outer god. Some people who were brought up in a religious home experienced trauma and alienation that resulted in a rejection of all external religious doctrine. This can later create obstacles to finding one's truth. An abused child may still find God, attesting to the deep spiritual drive that most children and adults possess.

Think of images that give you inspiration: Paul Bunyan chopping away negative thoughts with Babe the blue ox carting them away or the jolly green giant laughing as he stomps on each negative thought. Imagine yourself as bamboo swaying when stress rises then resuming a still, upright position as stress subsides. My life is like a garden where I plant beautiful vegetables and flowers and can easily recognize the weeds of distorted thoughts that I yank out of the earth. In *Six Seconds to True Calm*, Robert Simon Siegel writes of visualizing a little sun above your head beaming brightly then descending into your chest, joyous and happy; it protects you. The little sun is our center, holding our intuition and creativity. It is the healing light of God reaching into our being and bodies. "The path of the righteous is like the morning sun shining ever brighter till the full light

Chapter 4: Spirit Care

of day" (Prov. 4:18). "For with you is the fountain of life, in your light we see light" (Ps. 36:9).

But how exactly is the little sun accessed? First, by releasing any push to make it reveal itself. Breathe in deeply and slowly out to beckon the parasympathetic nervous system and invite intuition to come up as a new little shoot of sunlight, delicate and precious. Visualize the little sun in your chest filling up with life energy. Send good thoughts and feelings of a loved one, music, a beautiful place, or a passionate activity to the little sun to help it keep its light bright within you. Difficulty picturing and feeling the little sun is a reflection of the tenuous relationship between you and your true self. Just keep practicing seeing your little sun every day to identify more and more fully with your center, the place where you feel God most clearly. Gradually, inner negative dialogue diminishes and compassion takes its place. By freeing our energy to circulate within, we dissolve the blocking of anxiety, low self-image, and negativity. We stop energizing our anxieties and doubts. Our health thrives more fully. Turn on the little sun, and keep it turned on all the time. "I am the light of the world. Whoever follows me will never walk in darkness but will have the light of life" (John 8:12). Ask for help from intuition, then release all tension, so it will spontaneously rise and calm you.

So, let's do this. Write down everything that you feel, not think, is meaningful and sacred in your life. Contemplate upon this sacredness. When ready, ask for this sacredness to help you. Let this little seed begin to sprout within you, requiring only a drop of open-mindedness. Seek this little seed of awe that will diminish the growing magnet of anxiety within you and help you to deeply heal. It is our ultimate responsibility to quiet ourselves and connect with something higher in order to heal anxiety at its root. Finding a purposeful and benevolent meaning in life is as air is to the lungs. Having a belief in something beyond one's everyday ego can banish fear attacks of which relentless and destructive anxiety keeps pushing onto the center stage of the mind. Having a religion is not required to be spiritually fit. We come to understand God sometimes slowly, sometimes quickly.

Care of the spirit is a priority if you wish for the most far reaching healing and fulfillment in life. It asks to be prioritized and practiced in order to unfold and bloom, giving depth and richness to being alive. Spiritual health is a rudder for balanced and contemplative thinking. It is necessary to be able to differentiate whether a thought is coming from the anxiety disorder or whether a thought is coming from wisdom. When calm or not quite calm, simply ask, "Self, is this thought coming from illness or coming from wisdom? God, what do you think?" The intuitive, rational answer will come now or later in the day. Maybe even in a dream. Asking for help decreases the intolerance for uncertainty. Serotonin may now do its job of balancing the psyche more efficiently, and dysfunctional brain pathways will be less traveled by habitual impulses. Your wellbeing now pervades consciousness, and beauty is seen in the ordinary. Overwhelming uncertainty is lessened, and one can embrace what uncertainty that does appear in life and in our bodies as a spiritual gift, a mystery.

Fearaholism

The vise that anxiety and safety behaviors exert is similar to that of an addiction choking the life out of you. When an addiction and/or anxiety seeps or crashes into one's life, it takes on a stranglehold grip that is far greater than a mere bad habit. Because this grip defies normal efforts to free oneself, one has no other choice but to find something stronger than the stranglehold as well as oneself for healing to ensue. If you alone were able to break this hold and resolve this struggle, you would have done it a long time ago. An anxiety disorder may be thought of as fearaholism. A fearaholic cannot pick up the first catastrophic thought, as an alcoholic cannot pick up the first drink, without the debauchery starting up once again. Instead of one's fears wreaking havoc in life, a fearaholic can have dialogue with God or prayer to gain the strength to resist submerging into fear on a daily basis. Control attempts and fear are released onto something bigger—what a relief. Prayer utilizing beautiful, meaningful language aimed toward something higher, stronger, and finer along with honest self-searching can soothe the amygdala. A heartfelt and humble request for help and then following spiritual direction is the most effective treatment for addiction that exists. Millions have had their lives saved this way. Let go and let God, which is said by many recovering addicts.

In my twenty's, I fought to gain control over an addiction to food. I woke up one morning after hitting the food insanity wall again to finally ask if God, who I had forgotten about, could hear me and please help me to stop the out-of-control bingeing and purging madness. A sense of light filled my being. My room seemed brighter, and I felt a sweet and beautiful peace come over me. The obsession to go downstairs and eat two boxes of foodless food had vanished. This was nothing short of a miracle. Anxiety can be addressed the same way when you ask with all your heart for something greater than your everyday self to help you.

Chapter 4: Spirit Care

To be in acceptance and to be able to turn anxiety over to God may begin with clearly affirming every morning that your body is what it is: highly sensitive and reactive in mysterious ways, in baffling ways. You must acknowledge every day that you have an anxiety disorder that is very real while accepting the reality of risk, randomness, and uncertainty. To say: "I set my health worries aside and allow my body to do its work. I am okay in having a hypersensitive alarm system. I expect these expressions to happen." Instead of drowning in alarm, you recognize familiarity and attain serenity towards these sensations when they happen. And they will happen.

Here is a prayer one can say every morning:

"Dear God,

Please help me to remember I have a sensitive, reactive body every day. Help me remember its random, intermittent nature. Please help me to know this as deeply as I know I am alive. I absolutely have a sensitive, reactive body and have had it all my life and will keep having it for the rest of my life. This way I will remain at peace when sensations come and can give them to you.

Thank you,

Your Child."

Death Phobia

Much fear of illness is tightly entwined with the fear of dying and/or being dead. This is uncertainty to the max for many. Others feel confident about death, as it is explained by their religion's teachings. Many people fear that dying will mean severe pain amidst loss of everything that they love. Some are horrified of the possibility of becoming nothing for the rest of eternity. Being nothing for eternity—it's too much. However, others do not mind this fate. The glib quip of "Well, when you are dead, you won't be alive to fear anything so why fear it?" never worked for me. I'd still be dead, and I still don't like it.

Notice that we are asking this question of eternal nothingness based upon linear thinking. What about the eternity that happened before we were born? We got through that. Now, facing the future eternity, we need a deep desire to find something beyond infinite oblivion that will initiate an experiential faith in something else that goes beyond this linear thinking and provides precious comfort. At fourteen, I found myself deeply contemplating dying and being dead while sitting in an English class one day. The religion I was raised in felt useless to me now; there were too many contradictions and unanswered questions. I experienced a terrifying scenario—my soul fading into eternal nothingness. When consulting with others regarding this spiritual distress, most people reflexively responded, "Well, you're dead, so what does it matter?" This response drove me deeper into despair. Others asserted I would go to heaven if I lived a good life on earth. Both gave me no substance or comfort, and people seemed more and more robotic to me. Life events and routines provided distraction and served as a Band-Aid for this despair and existential hell.

Decades later, I recognized the catastrophic thinking error of this adolescent girl contemplating death. I realized that that terrifying scenario of being swallowed up into nothingness forever was only ONE option. Such wall hitting experiences may serve as beacons to go deeper in one's spiritual walk rather than being some huge gong dooming you forever into oblivion. I still wish that an angel or wise person had taught me that dissolving into nothingness was only one option and that another option existed—transcending death. One divine man resumed life after He died, which was witnessed by hundreds of people. He then rose up. This was and is something to deeply contemplate, religious or not. Being swallowed up into eternal deadness and/or hell is incongruent with divine order and a loving Creator, who has known you even before you were born (Psalm 139: 13-16).

Only spiritual fitness will give us meaning and peace regarding death. Where is your deepest sense of self that can make peace with death leading you? In stillness and quietness may we hear the answer.

Let's keep talking about how to attain spiritual fitness. Since the body and soul are not separate, let's start with the body, move into the mind at work, and then conclude with the serenity of a quiet mind.

Move It, Baby

The human body has 640 or more muscles (depending on how they are counted) that are made to contract and relax in order to move the skeleton, organs, blood vessels, and heart. The hardest working muscle is the heart. The busiest muscles work the eye. The soleus muscle below the calf muscle pulls with the greatest force against gravity when walking, running, and dancing, in an effort to keep the body upright. And even when sleeping, the tongue pushes saliva down the throat and keeps us from choking. Do we ever thank these beautiful, hardworking muscles for all they do for us? Let us do that now. Exercising these muscles that cry to flex and stretch

Chapter 4: Spirit Care

is essential. Why? Besides increasing immunity, decreasing inflammation, maintaining arterial elasticity, decreasing brain shrinkage and memory loss, keeping blood flowing smoothly, increasing neurogenesis (especially in the hippocampus responsible for memory and learning), strengthening bones, improving insulin resistance, and sweating to clear toxins from the skin (the second kidney), exercise acts to clear the mind, releasing tension and decreasing depression. Exercise decreases stress hormones while endorphins (the brain's own calming and pain reducing chemicals), serotonin and norepinephrine are increased. Exercise can bring on a blissful state known as the endorphin rush. I experienced this pleasant state while training for a run-walk marathon and suddenly understood the penchant for running nearly every day. Experiencing that blissful peace of mind dissociated from any negative thinking was a serendipitous moment, and I plan to keep running until I die.

Have you had any thoughts about dropping dead while running a marathon as some highly fit (on the outside) athletes have done? Let's get clear about it now and have no fear. As Dr. Mercola writes, the heart is not meant to go up from pumping five quarts of blood per minute when sitting to twenty-five quarts per minute when vigorously exercising day after day. The volume overload stretches the walls of heart muscle, breaking fibers apart and leading to inflammation, plaque buildup, scarring, rhythm disturbances, and enlargement of the heart that interferes with blood filling the chambers properly. Intense exercise also increases cortisol levels that then depresses immune functioning and promotes insomnia. OK, well then, what? Most days, not every day, run forty-five minutes at a pace that you can carry on a conversation. Reduce high blood pressure and get rid of fatty, insulin, and sugar-laden blood with a plant diet so inflammation and arterial plaque buildup will be much less likely to rupture and clot, cutting off blood flow to tissue. Then run high! Run high and fearlessly in the sunshine and fresh air, near water (especially moving water like oceans and waterfalls) and trees. Rule in recovery: exercise or be stiff with angry arteries.

Negative ions are molecules that are abundant near moving water, thunderstorms, and sunshine. They decrease with the full moon, dry days, dust, and smoke. When inhaled, negative ions lift mood and give energy. Once in the blood stream, they produce a chemical reaction that increases serotonin levels and increase oxygen to the brain (sunlight increases dopamine and serotonin, so why not get two for one?). A stale, fluorescently lit office and/or air conditioning type of environment produces positive ions that are draining, creating a need to escape to the negative ions. Even being around plants and taking showers increases negative ions. So when feeling depleted, go to the beach, walk and run barefoot, breathe deeply, and fill up on the glories of nature.

Spirituality is not static—do something. Even if it's meditating for three hours, do something. Rumi wrote: "When you do things from your soul, you feel a river moving in you, a joy." Deliberately working the body dissipates tension. Move your body in a way that you enjoy such as yoga, dance, running, smashing a ball with tennis, swimming, hiking, or tai chi. Commit to doing this exhilarating activity on a routine basis, at least a few times a week. No matter how much a person tries to ditch their way out of exercising, there are no excuses for not moving. For anyone. If you reject all exercise as something that just ain't your bag, well, it wouldn't be surprising that there is some anxiety or depression lingering within. Is food tasteless or you just can't stop eating chocolate and you're lying awake in the middle of the night and sleeping all day? Do you feel less energetic about life; in fact, does it feel grim and grey? Please follow brain care and talk to someone about feeling so empty and sad for too long. Then force yourself to kick, jump, or canter, as exercise increases serotonin levels and helps defeat depression. Check out if there is some deep-seated laziness that needs to be blown up out of the water. Some problems have to be told to suck it up, and spiritual laziness is no exception.

Try this: when anxiety hits, thwart it by breaking out into singing opera, belting out a prayer, or moving your body vigorously to lasso the energy of anxiety before the anxiety gains momentum. I mean, dance with every bit of passion you have. "David was dancing before the Lord with all his might" (2 Sam. 6:14). The energy of anxiety has got to go somewhere once it starts, so let it fly out of you through a gesture of passion. Here it comes; there it goes, goodbye.

And then there's the brain. We need to work our frontal lobe like a dog who loves to dig, as this frontal lobe languishes without purpose, drive, or focus. The idle, not to be confused with peaceful, brain is anxiety's playground. Therefore, exercising our frontal lobe and the rest of our brain by practicing something skillful helps to thwart anxiety. Redeeming activities like hobbies, meaningful work, and playing music serve as a distraction to anxious rumination and help forge nerve pathways that support wellbeing and full living. Neil Nedley, MD, states that exercising the frontal lobe with prayer, meaningful discussions, thoughtful reading, classical music, hobbies, and activities that involve contemplative thinking keep the frontal lobe engaged and able to prevent and cope with

Chapter 4: Spirit Care 111

anxiety and depression. Even working with your hands stimulates frontal lobe activity.

Activities such as prayer and meditation, soothing words, visualization, deep abdominal breathing (counting or breathing slowly when an alarm goes off helps the cortex to catch up and calmly evaluate the impression), being with friends, laughter, music, journaling, yoga, and non-extreme exercise along with an attitude of self-confidence, fortitude, and resilience all help to balance cortisol levels and strengthen the frontal lobe. When the threat passes and cortisol levels diminish, the parasympathetic nervous system resumes and calms the body and mind down. The PFC of the frontal lobe may then step up to its rightful place as leader of this pack. Avoid what suppresses frontal lobe functioning (booming syncopated music, rapid screen images, etc.) that provide explosive entertainment and a trance-like interaction with the screen. Excessive entertainment screen viewing can become strongly habitual, as staring at the tube releases continual dopamine that suppresses frontal lobe activity. As a result, natural rewards are less rich and meaningful (Binus 2016).

Ask how much you are working your frontal lobe. How much are you titillating your limbic system with entertainment screen viewing, high drama in life, and eating too much food? TV does not expand the brain like creativity or working to reach a goal does. It is obvious that horror shows depicting someone around your age dying from some rare disease or some scary thing coming with a knife has got to go. We are talking anxiety management: avoiding negative stimuli and diving into positive activities, which work the frontal lobe and tone down negative reactivity. Guard your frontal lobe from non-redeeming input such as gossip, negativity, trash media, and unhealthy people. Remember the omega-3 foods, plants, and sunlight. Move, laugh, write, sing—stimulate a release of serotonin that will help form positive brain pathways. Be with those who you love and love you. Whenever I hold my dogs close and tell them how much I love them, I always feel a lessening of anxiety (augmented by oxytocin, the bonding and anxiety-lessening hormone).

Writing, from journaling to poetry, lends clarity and imparts objectivity from inexorable worriment like no other activity. Writing clarifies successes, increases motivation, insight, and stimulates creativity. Try writing a poem about living with anxiety. I did once and saw my body as a tempestuous ocean. I was a little boat bobbing on the surface above great fish, coral, volatile waves, and overwhelming depths. Despite the simultaneous submission towards the wind, the sun and pollutants dumped into my ocean, I said, "I will calmly put up sails, row, and remain a finger's rudder of navigation, weathering the storms and drifting upon an emerald bay."

Just forget about whether you can dance or sing or write. Do it anyway and see the hidden creativity that has always been within you becoming another tool to keep anxiety where it belongs.

Calm and Quiet Within

Sensitive to dysfunction and imbalance, the brain quickly signals to the mind when something is wrong: "Self? This is the brain. Something is up; help me fix it." If my mind is frantic, tense, scattered, or lethargic, it will be less able to listen as keenly to more subtle messages. Our fast-paced culture in the USA is viewed as the norm. We drive like maniacs on the freeway going eighty miles per hour, sneaking a quick call or text on our cell phones, breaking the law twice. People can be immersed in technology to the point of walking into traffic while staring and punching into a small handheld screen. Does anyone realize that this is not healthy or normal? Are we powerless over these seemingly inevitable stressors? Must we live with a frequently irritated brain and exhausted adrenals? No, even though we feel compelled to go, go, go and do, do, do. Overstimulation and multi-tasking is not something of which to be proud. But neither is being sedentary. Both suppress frontal lobe activity that then defaults to the limbic system, which takes over and gives anxiety free reign. Anxiety is attracted to the frantic state, while a healthy body is geared to be relaxed and peaceful most of the time. Stop now and ask, "Is my brain spinning? Am I tense, anxious, or condemning myself?" Yes? Just stop and breathe. "Am I absorbing toxic people and negativity? Trying to do too much?" Become aware of this possible adrenaline habit, breathe, and get out. Remember, a non-frantic brain is more receptive to the quieting and calming effects of GABA and serotonin.

"Serenity is not freedom from the storm, but peace amid the storm" (author unknown). What interferes with managing inner chaos and maintaining peace amid the storm? Is it the job, junk talking, wasting time, trash eating, not knowing what you are doing, injustice, or irritating people? Day and night, every frantic, fearful, or angry feeling and negative thought triggers the amygdala with the adrenal glands spewing epinephrine and cortisol into circulation, increasing blood pressure, heart rate, breathing, muscle tension, and gastro-intestinal upset. There goes the relaxation, right down the chute. No matter that health advice repeatedly encourages everyone to work humane hours and get enough sleep, step-

Chapter 4: Spirit Care 113

ping up to work frequent extra shifts is still seen as a noble and committed act of loyalty with many people throwing themselves to work more, more, more. This self-created stress can be disguised with the excuse that "I am a hard worker and not a quitter." or "Stand by your man!" or just plain "I need the money." Some people are brave enough to buck this value and prioritize quietness, rest, and having fun along with hard work to protect resiliency and wellbeing.

As you move through the day, do you feel energized and efficient or that you are in a duel with time, feeling frantic and tense? How busy do you like to be? Pacing yourself to manage time and space according to what your nervous system can handle helps prevent anxiety blowouts. From staring into space to frenetically cleaning the house while trying to compose a speech, each person has a congruency within this continuum. The mind seeks to remain within this congruency to avoid brain chaos, dysphoria, and shut down. How do you like the space around you to be arranged? Clutter and chaos with piles, disarray, and disorganization is a form of overstimulation causing an impasse in your life. As Marie Kondo writes, if any object does not bring a spark of joy, let it go. Could the same be said for how one manages time and carrying out tasks? We know that subtle little forms of hoarding are not a friend of a peaceful and centered life, so what about subtle little forms of wasting time? When we can dispose of mental clutter, we gain mental energy to allow inner calm and a more finely-tuned attention.

Being quiet and calm within is not synonymous with inertia or laziness. Someone may have inner calm and at the same time be alert and productive. Inertia may be a relaxed state, but it lacks the precious quality of attention. Deliberate attention, of which we need to tame inner chaos, is quite different from being glued to a tube. The thing is you just can't snap your fingers like a genie and order your brain to be quiet. Don't think, "OK, I can just sit and meditate (secretly go to sleep)...." No, meditation requires an erect back and focused mind.

Meditation requires the brain to shift into a dominance of slower brain waves to access quietness. Brain waves are synchronized electrical pulses from groups of neurons communicating with each other. The brain is an electrochemical organ and our mind regulates its activities by means of these electric waves that vary from fast to slow frequencies. Our brain waves and daily experiences are inseparable.

These waves include:

- Gamma: fastest waves, consolidation of learning and processing of information from different brain areas. REM sleep. Too much: frantic, off the wall state; too little: ADHD, depression, learning disabilities.

- Beta: awake, alert, engaged in mental activities, socializing, reading. Learn to do this without coffee. A plant diet provides more energy to think and plan and do. Too much: anxiety, agitation, and insomnia; too little: ADHD, depression, diminished thinking. Caffeine and other stimulants increase both gamma and beta waves.

- Alpha: relaxed alertness that allows meditation, intuition, and enhanced learning to happen. The brain may be calmed by endorphins and the parasympathetic nervous system. If one remains in high beta too long, alpha blocking occurs, and one just can't relax. Alpha waves are increased by alcohol, marijuana, and some antidepressants. Fervently focusing on a lecture in beta then escaping to walk in a beautiful garden would release beta into alpha waves.

- Theta: daydreaming and dreaming sleep, hypnotic states, intuition, connected to emotions, creativity. Too much: depression, can't focus; too little: anxiety and poor emotional awareness.

- Delta: slowest waves found in deep, dreamless sleep, deep meditation states, and unconsciousness. When the body is able to do the most healing and why restorative sleep is essential to the healing process. Too much: inability to think, severe ADHD; too little: unable to rejuvenate the body, poor sleep. Depressant drugs increase both theta and delta waves.

Although one brain wave may predominate at any given time, other brain waves are present in a mix at all times. Fatigue, pain, drugs, emotional distress, and stress can imbalance brain wave functioning. Instabilities in brain rhythms can lead to tics, obsessive compulsive disorder, attention deficit hyperactivity disorder (ADHD), aggression, anxiety, panic, bipolar disorder, migraine headaches, narcolepsy, epilepsy, and vertigo.

Calmness and mental flexibility enable transitioning through different brain waves resulting in stress management, focused attention, sleeping, meditation, and spiritual awareness. We seek the alpha state to initiate and deepen meditation, and we practice meditation to beckon the alpha

Chapter 4: Spirit Care

state to take us into peacefulness. Activities that promote a quiescent mind and a sense of serenity evoke the alpha state. Centering the mind with slow, deep breaths, relaxing each muscle starting with the scalp when drifting off to sleep, being present in the moment, prayer, calming music, and yoga facilitate moving from higher to lower frequencies, activating different areas of the brain and allowing more time between thoughts to control impulsiveness of thought or behavior.

It is critical for one to set aside time each day to focus and center. John C. Maxwell wrote: "You'll never change your life until you change something you do daily. The secret of your success is found in your daily routine." Otherwise more primitive brain patterns will just have their way with you: an overly sensitive amygdala, circuitous caudates, excessive stress hormones, and habituated negative brain pathways. Begin by simply accepting any anxiety in the moment and breathe out its tension, noting the intrusiveness and bias of those negative thoughts. This is known as mindfulness and being present in the moment. As James Baraz has stated, "Mindfulness is simply being aware of what's happening right now minus reactions as wishing it were different. To enjoy pleasant moments without holding on when it changes (it will) and endure unpleasant moments without fearing it will always be this way (it won't)." Mindfulness allows the peaceful parasympathetic nervous system to work unhindered and promotes intuitive awareness. How do we interrupt this associative domino action of the mind and create space for receiving this energy? In the morning before the compelling rush of a new day creeps or roars in ("Oh, I need to make tea first. Oh, I need to empty the dryer, now sweep, what time is it, I have to hurry"), sit with your back straight and direct attention upon each part of your body and your breathing. Breathe out any tension and go to the most sacred place in your being where the awareness of I AM quietly exists: "Be still and know that I am God" (Ps. 46:10). When you begin to focus, strengthening all attention on breathing or body alignment during a state of quietness creates space to separate from habitual negative thinking. It transforms a self-belief of fear, doubt, and insecurity into the truth that sets me free, as mentioned in the Gospel of John. Try for one minute to sustain attention in mindfulness then extend these moments and clear all health concerns. Practice again before going to sleep as well as deep breathing at least twice a day and as needed. Within the silence one may recite sacred words such as God, truth, love, or strength. Ask the source of goodness, God, for the serenity to accept the things one cannot change, the courage to change the things one can, and wisdom to know the difference (The Serenity Prayer). The answer will come when you let go and focus on the quiet that yearns to be heard.

All around us is something higher and finer—an energy that provides illumination and serenity. It can lift us from limited and negative mind states. Though our heavy, coarse and mechanical egos interfere with accessing this finer energy, we may work to become quiet enough to access a centered sense of holiness filled with God's light—my little sun. This is a very sweet and quiet place of stillness.

Thoreau once wrote: "If a man does not keep pace with his companions perhaps it is because he hears a different drummer. Let him step to the music which he hears however measured or far away." We come to abide in God's word (truth) and "know the truth and the truth will set you free" (John 8:32) at our own pace. Ironically, vulnerability is our strength. Meditate upon this and "Whatsoever things are true, honest, just, pure, lovely, good; if there be any virtue and praise, think on these things" (Phil. 4:8).

It has been said that in order for cloudy water to clear, it must sit quietly for a moment. Fearful rumination keeps shaking this jar of chaotic anxiety and thwarting the clarity of insight and discernment from quietly coming into awareness. The answers do not come when the mind is busy but rather when the mind is still. Intuition means learning from within. We must sense the pathway to heal the mind and spirit and replace superstitious and negative "What if?" thinking with inspired thinking. Much of our thinking is reflexive. How much of our thinking grapples with such subjects as ethics, aesthetics, or existentialism? Being quiet allows time and space for contemplative thinking and intuition to whisper its truth to you. To become silent amidst chaos allows something stronger than our common egos to be heard. The quieter you become, the more you can hear a Spirit of holiness calling to you. The tremendous relief of deeply trusting this inner feeling grows stronger in time.

Intuition speaks quietly with symbols and feelings. Allow them to emerge and listen to their inner meaning as though you were studying a poem to understand its message and art. Close your eyes, breathe out all tension, and ask for an image to come to you. Describe this image with as much detail as you can. Do not trust a sudden fearful image, as that is the language of anxiety. One morning while running with my dogs, I had a sudden image of encountering some strange, aggressive dogs. I quickly asked, "Is this an intuitive warning or random, superstitious thinking?" Discerning this question, I noticed the warning thought had a little pricking intrusiveness. This quality of thought did not appear worthy of serious consideration, so I set out to defy the fear and kept going. No such conflict manifested. I knew then that anxiety has a twitch-like, jabbing quality, while intuition is felt more profoundly like a heart beating steadily, often with a loving nature within its message.

The blessing of intuitive knowing may come spontaneously without conscious effort. One evening while meeting with friends, a man walking a dog came by and asked if any of us belonged to this dog. No, none of us did. The man could not keep her and was going to try to find her home, and if not, he would just release her into the streets. He walked on with her. I worried about her safety and wondered if I should take this dog home. A short period later, I felt a wave of relief and joy sweep over me, sensing that this dog was now safe. "What?" my left brain asked, "How do you know?" My right brain declared, "It's true." After the gathering, I went to the man's house and learned that she had been reunited with her guardian! Very relieved for this dear dog, I began to ponder that I had experienced a clear intuitive gift of awareness. Not a spectacular example of intuition, but it was a transcendent knowing nevertheless. My nerve pathways switched into a serendipitous sense that this is the mind I am supposed to live from, my real mind. My left brain exclaimed, "You are capable of these transcendent verities, and by God, you will stay in them!" My dependence upon my God-given intuition took a soaring leap.

There is a calmer part of me that is expanding. Mental gear shifting and brakes depend on becoming quiet enough to allow the mind to hear intuitive wisdom regarding a sensation, knowing that you are safe. Once this precious gift from God speaks do not second-guess it. It's like asking for reassurance from someone over and over, burning both you and them out, while health anxiety is doing push-ups. Rule in recovery: do not second-guess intuition. Stay in the present moment and allow catastrophic thoughts to pass through without engaging them. This weakens their grip. This is what we want! Victory!

Dance of Tapping

Energy techniques, such as the Emotional Freedom Technique (EFT), utilizes gentle rhythm of fingers tapping certain meridian points or energy channels along the body while speaking honest and loving words. Tapping can promote alpha brain wave frequencies that help create a new normal thinking pattern including intuitive awareness. Based on ancient Chinese acupressure and modern psychology, tapping works to intercept the amygdala's firing of "What if?" catastrophic, nonstop messages towards the frontal lobe. It also helps remove the charge of bad memories that continue to feed the fear circuit.

Begin tapping along the fleshy side of the hand while stating, "Even though I have (anxiety, fibromyalgia, pain, etc.), I love and accept myself completely." Next, tap on the eye orbit, under the nose, chin, chest where shoulder blades begin, under the arm on the side of the chest, and on top of the head. Repeat the statement each time. Combining tapping as suggested by Nick Ortner, author of *The Tapping Solution*, with obsessive-compulsive redirection skills, as written by Dr. Schwartz, one could say:

> Even though my anxiety disorder/OCD is sending a false message and furthering a neuro-chemical imbalance and dysfunctional circuit in my brain, I deeply love and accept myself. Even though I feel afraid with a compulsive urge to scan and check, I deeply love and accept myself. I know this false message is not real, and I trust my intuition/God's hand/Jesus' healing light. Even though I feel this panic, I love and accept myself, and it is safe to relax and release this panic. I need things to change now; my body shouldn't act up like this. I am so used to this panic, but it is only holding me back from clarity and true peace. Maybe things are unfolding as they should; maybe this is all leading me to something great. I have God's love within me now. I know what's right for me. I am creating room for a miracle—I feel joy and excitement with this new space and ability. Even if I don't know the answer now, the answer will come. Maybe I am exactly where I am meant to be. I am connecting with my core right here and right now. As I quiet this panic, intuition appears, and I know what is right for me. I breathe out any remaining panic, and I breathe in peace and truth. My body is striving for health and healing every minute. I am protected by plants and by God (who created these plants), and I can handle my life (Ortner 2013).

Hearing yourself speak these words of sanity and prayer helps to expose the little goblin of anxiety hiding behind the curtain.

Know the Truth and Be Free

True victories in life are achieved with passion and sustained effort. What may bring ease and exhilaration, such as fortune, looks or talent, will not build true depth and richness within our beings. These luxuries lead to hedonic adaptation and are unsustainable sources of happiness. Plants that many cannot or will not bring themselves to delectably consume have the sun's energy within them that sustains life on this earth. The answer is not antibiotics, sedatives, money, antidepressants, or romantic interludes. The drive to consume intensely stimulating food in order to enjoy eating is the road of the easier, softer way. The truth is that the easier, softer way will not provide enduring health, let alone long lasting fortitude and priceless piece of mind. Neglecting spiritual needs or approaching spiritual needs in a superficial manner leads to a deep, gnawing existential pain that can gnaw away at your life. It can then become automatic to reach for a drug or chase materialism, addictive hits, or some other distraction to fill the existential void. These pursuits not only fail but they also worsen spiritual emptiness and yearning to feel something within. This is our true longing that lies beneath outer chasing: to live from the wholeness within our spirit.

As people working to contain anxiety, we know that we cannot afford catastrophic ruminations, and we need to place these types of thoughts off limits. Myrtle Fillmore (1845–1931), co-founder of Unity Christian Church, contracted tuberculosis at a young age and spent many years believing she was incurably weak and sickly. Upon hearing a metaphysician speak of the innate potential for divine healing through the use of affirmative prayer, she began to proclaim, "I am a child of God, and therefore, I do not inherit sickness." This message of truth transformed her body, mind, and spirit, and along with adopting a plant-based diet, cured her tuberculosis. Yes. And I am a child of God, and I didn't inherit anxiety taking over my life either. When an anxious thought comes up, we can respond with affirmative prayer and know the truth that sets us free. A warm, enlightening message of the God's infinite illumination is always with us.

Raise your right hand and repeat after me, "I am blessed with intuition and healing tools that enable me to handle whatever life gives me, pleasurable or painful. My right brain and left pre-frontal cortex are in full control now, rich with vivid life energy and ever-present intuition. I love God, life, and myself." Intuition is a crown of spirituality and a blessing from God that guides, protects, and illuminates. Blindness receives light, and deafness hears music. Clarity is granted to discern obnoxious "what-if" false warnings from what is rational and what is felt in the heart. Intuition knows the whole truth, the full truth, and nothing but the truth of the body and mind. Listen for intuition and know your stronger, Higher Power has a plan for you, and that plan is to be victorious.

Bravery Heals

Fear. You gotta love it. In 1987, Susan Jeffers wrote *Feel the Fear and Do It Anyway* to proclaim the truth that taking up your courage when afraid will bless your soul with knowing that you can handle whatever comes your way. I can avouch for the triumph of standing up to the fear and walking through it. Once while trying to gather the courage to travel 300 miles to attend a health conference, I kept feeling waves of doom and doubt with nearly everything in me fighting to not go on this trip. I knew it was a shred of agoraphobia and remembered "feel the fear and do it anyway" to gather some gumption to boot myself out of the house and go to the thing. But wait, shouldn't facing the fear feel noble and enlightening? This struggle just stunk, nothing pretty about it. "I can't do it!" I wailed again and again. Somehow, I put one foot in front of the other and just set out to do it, even if somewhat catatonically. Yeah!

I am so grateful to this day that I did not cave into the fear, as I was richly blessed with a deep, God-given knowing that I had and have secretly won this fear battle! That something deep inside of my heart is stronger than this anxiety disorder! Plus, I was able to meet the greatest health teacher of all time, Michael Greger, MD, author of *How Not To Die* (2015) and creator of NutritionFacts.org. This incredible guiding light of health, who as a child watched his grandmother rise from her death chair of heart disease after adopting a plant diet and living thirty-one more years, would grow up to become the great healing physician that he is today. Speaking with Dr. Greger that day, I felt awed by his radiance and kindness. It hit me that here he is flying all over the country, even sailing on ships to teach and spread the message of health and healing, while I struggled with a mere 300 miles. You know that saying "Get over yourself"? I did feel quite a wake-up call in that moment. I came home elated with a new quiet strength.

No one with a heart and uncalcified amygdala is immune to anxiety. Deeply spiritual people can suffer bouts of anxiety. Those of us who are highly sensitive may feel overwhelmed by the abject and nearly infinite suffering in this world. We know that we are vulnerable to unbearable suffering, too. This disturbing awareness increases the risk of sliding into despair and depression. Can suffering from health anxiety also lead one to nose-dive into this black place? Oh, yes. Is the human will, strong as it is,

Chapter 4: Spirit Care

strong enough to keep this risk of black depression at bay? Well, no. Try telling someone who is depressed to snap out of it. It won't work. Either we open to something boundless and beautiful beyond ourselves or suffer mercilessly.

Do not many of us seek to find the transmundane? Why is it that belief and experiences of God result in transformations of body, mind, and spirit? To refuse this spiritual humility stems from great self-absorption. To wallow in ruminations of suffering now or in the future is also a form of self-absorption. "Why do we suffer?" we lament. "And why does God seem to allow suffering?" Do you think that God is a large man who capriciously runs the show granting some wishes while ignoring others? Maybe the relationship between God and suffering has to do with that of transforming one's being through suffering—going through pain means something deeper is strengthened within us. Hardship can be a pathway to peace. Trust intuition and surrender to uncertainty, even embrace it. When things are very difficult, know you're on the verge of a breakthrough. To bravely endure suffering begins a refinement process in one's soul. Or as many have phrased it: that which doesn't kill you will make you stronger.

Because those upon a spiritual path have developed a rich base of spiritual comfort and wisdom, they don't spin as long in catastrophic doom thinking and are able to come out of it wiser and stronger. Something is there for us. So, when you go through deep waters, I will be with you (see Isa. 43:2).

Persistence, viewed as the greatest force in accomplishment, needs to be bravely practiced each time as you face anxiety. Rumi once wrote: "Come, come whoever you are, wanderer, worshiper, lover of leaving, it doesn't matter. Ours is not a caravan of despair. Come, even if you have broken your vow a hundred times. Come, come again, come." Rebuke the spirit of fear and order it to get behind you with every attack (see Matt. 16:23). Fear is a stumbling block containing the things of humanity and not of God. Be persistent as you center within to gain awareness of something deeper in you that knows: "The lamp of the body is the eye. If the eye is single the whole body will be full of light." (Matt. 6:22; Luke 11:34).

Go to your core, pick up your sword, and with all the determination you have, stand up to this disorder. Be brave. You will win. Even now you are winning.

Don't Do This

When one is in the throes of out of control terror, fearing disease and/or death, all these suggestions can seem like wisps in the wind. One can feel hopeless and despair of ever being free of this fear curse. But "don't allow your wounds to transform you into something you are not" (Paulo Coelho). When despairing, one can only stop, breathe, and wait in the space where God's voice is heard. We can remember that our intuition has not died, and when the storm has passed, it will speak again, bringing comfort and guidance. Writing a letter to yourself when you feel strong and calm and then reading it the next time you feel this fear and despair is a prayer that can pull you out of the despair. It is said that God will not give you more than you can handle and that you were given this life because you are strong enough to live it. "You never realize how strong you are until being strong is the only choice you have" (Bob Marley).

Michael Evans, a British author who wrote *How to Beat Health Anxiety*, stood up to disturbing and uncomfortable sensations, such as skipping heart beats, shooting head pain, or waves of nausea, exclaiming, "OK, head pain, do your worst. Go ahead and kill me!" His acceptance of sensations with massive embracing of uncertainty ironically transformed uncertainty into a certainty and gave him healing from health anxiety. This is similar to the story of David (who could symbolize the frontal lobe and intuition) and Goliath (who could represent an anxiety disorder). Of course Goliath was much bigger and stronger than David, yet David slew this mean giant and became king of Israel. People have been able to detach from abject conditions during war, enduring the unbearable and making it to the other side. This is your story now. As Michael Evans further states, the worst and scariest thing is to crawl through an unlived, anxiety-ridden life. So, don't do this. Victories over fear build upon themselves and diminish intolerance for uncertainty. Recovery happens. To you.

Health anxiety can heal quickly or slowly. It is highly treatable, but it requires practice and commitment to nourish and retrain the brain and spiritualize the mind. Rather than cure, one learns to accept having a fallible and expressive body as well as a sensitive mind in a randomized and painful world that has streams of beauty calling to you. Embrace and live exuberantly in these streams of beauty. Because health anxiety can be more or less chronic, you better have something to guide you as a raft does on rapid waters. Develop your own relapse prevention plan that encompasses your new healing lifestyle. What is in your anxiety healing toolbox for your brain, your mind, and your spirit? Your tool box might include

Chapter 4: Spirit Care

meditation, dream study, prayer, a whole foods plant-based diet, fasting, deliberate breathing, counseling, medications for emergencies, meaningful work, and connecting with those who you love both two-footed and four-footed. Life's trials, tribulations, and temptations are very powerful in seducing and returning one to that bleak, fear-ridden level of consciousness. It is so easy to slip back into experiencing that chronic and irrational fear. Relapse is possible if old behaviors and thinking errors are allowed to creep back in with nothing protecting oneself.

So, this is what we can do: 1) go to sleep before midnight and wake with the sun, 2) sit early in the morning to pray and seek inner quiet while being aware of posture, limbs, and breathing, 3) remember that intuition is always by my side, 4) that I will not fail to notice a real problem in my reactive mind and body, 5) run, dance, do yoga, 6) take the herbs ashwagandha and valerian, 6) eat plants and avoid consuming meat and dairy products, 7) fast every day, and 8) kiss, laugh, and talk with those we love.

As recovery progresses, one can tolerate more exposure to stimuli that used to set off the fear cascade thinking rut. A fear thought comes and is diverted into "I will not fail to notice a true problem" or "Go ahead and kill me" or "I listen to God and my intuition—not an anxiety disorder." There is acceptance of having good days and challenging days. It is important to know that when setbacks occur, they do not mean health anxiety recovery is hopeless. You just get back in the ring as quickly as you can, for you will win. Even then you are winning. You will no longer be bullied by health anxiety.

Something bigger has a plan for you; let go into that intelligence and power. Do you believe that everything is going to turn out all right? Yes. I am not going to cave into a lifeless life; I am going to live my life to the fullest.

The Magnificent Truth

"Everything you want is on the other side of fear" (Jack Canfield). Understanding health anxiety, committing to an uplifting way of life, and maintaining a connection with God will save you. From hell. The hell that is in us on earth and not the hell as described in the Bible. We become aware of our ability to choose silence versus chaotic noise; intuition versus reflexive mind; God's higher law versus unpredictable mishaps; and resilience versus intolerance of risk. We can let go and let God, just for today. Claim those sun-kissed plants as they flood your body with rich healing.

Claim your healing of this anxiety disorder every day. Know that the truth of God is always by your side.

As I gazed at my hand in the sunlight so long ago, a feeling of "I AM" emerged, a realization that I really, truly exist came to light for the first time in my young little brain. It was a moment of grace and beauty. A moment that would span throughout my life as the anchoring witness of God's light. A sacred moment beyond illusions and mishaps of life (like an anxiety disorder). So let's know that "unless you are converted and become as little children, you will never enter the kingdom of heaven" (Matt. 18:3).

May I end this on a note of my own faith? In the story of the Garden of Eden, there were only plants to feed the new humans, no animal flesh, no alien breast milk, no stoves or chemical food processing present. The new humans walked in the beauty of God's creation free of any anxiety. "You shall know the Truth and the Truth shall make you free" (John 8:32). "God has not given us a spirit of fear; but of power, and love, and of a sound mind." (2 Tim. 1:17). Jesus is my Healer for all eternity. He radiates such massive healing power. He resurrected others and Himself from the dead, which no other human has ever done. He healed many people from maladies of body, mind, and soul. I am safe with Him, my Shepherd.

References

Anderson, Mike. *Healing Cancer From Inside Out*. 2009. http://1ref.us/gk.

Arden, John B. *The Heal Your Anxiety Workbook New Techniques for Moving from Panic to Inner Peace*. Beverly, MA: Fair Winds Press, 2009.

Aron, Elaine N. *The Highly Sensitive Person How to Thrive When the World Overwhelms You*. New York: Broadway Books, 1997.

Bergland, Christopher. "How Does the Vagus Nerve Convey Gut Instincts to the Brain?" Psychology Today (blog), May 23, 2014. http://1ref.us/gl

Bergland, Christopher. "The Neurobiology of Grace Under Pressure." *Psychology Today* (blog), February 2, 2013. http://1ref.us/gm.

Berk, Michael, Lana J. Williams, Felice N. Jacka, Adrienne O'Neil, Julie A. Pasco, Steven Moylan, Nicholas B. Allen, Amanda L. Stuart, Amie C. Hayley, Michelle L. Byrne, and Michael Maes. "So Depression Is an Inflammatory Disease, but Where Does the Inflammation Come From?" *BMC Medicine BMC Med* 11, no. 1 (2013). doi:10.1186/1741-7015-11-200.

Binus, Daniel. "Media, Screens, and Mental Illness." Lecture, Emotional Summit Seminar, Weimar, CA, February, 2016.

Bleyer, Archie, and H. Gilbert Welch. "Effect of Three Decades of Screening Mammography on Breast-Cancer Incidence." *New England Journal of Medicine* 367, no. 21 (2012): 1998-2005. doi:10.1056/nejmoa1206809.

Campbell, T. Colin, and Thomas M. Campbell. *The China Study: The Most Comprehensive Study of Nutrition Ever Conducted and the Startling Implications for Diet, Weight Loss and Long-term Health*. Dallas, TX: BenBella Books, 2005.

Cherry, Neil. "Schumann Resonances, a Plausible Biophysical Mechanism for the Human Health Effects of Solar/Geomagnetic Activity." Human Sciences Department Lincoln University, New Zealand, September 6, 2002, http://1ref.us/gn.

Diagnostic and Statistical Manual of Mental Disorders: *DSM-5*. Washington, DC: American Psychiatric Association, 2013.

Evans, Michael. *How to Beat Health Anxiety*. Kindle E-book, 2013.

Greger, Michael. "A Better Way to Boost Serotonin." *NutritionFacts.org* (video blog), April 3, 2012. http://1ref.us/go.

Greger, Michael. "Do Vitamin D Supplements Help with Diabetes, Weight Loss and Blood pressure?" *NutritionFacts.org* (video blog), June 29, 2016. http://1ref.us/gp.

Greger, Michael. "Gut Dysbiosis: Starving Our Microbial Self." *NutritionFacts.org* (video blog), June 15, 2016. http://1ref.us/gq.

Greger, Michael. "Should We All Get Colonoscopies starting at age 50?" *NutritionFacts.org* (video blog), November 25, 2015. http://1ref.us/gr.

Greger, Michael. "The Best Way to get Vitamin D; Sun, Supplements or Salons?" *NutritionFacts.org* (video blog), July 8, 2016. http://1ref.us/gs.

Greger, Michael. "The Optimal Dose for Vitamin D Based on Natural Levels." *NutritionFacts.org* (video blog), July 6, 2016. http://1ref.us/gt.

Greger, Michael. "Will You Live Longer if you take Vitamin D Supplements?" *NutritionFacts.org* (video blog), July 1, 2016. http://1ref.us/gu.

References

Greger, Michael, and Gene Stone. *How Not to Die: Discover the Foods Scientifically Proven to Prevent and Reverse Disease*. New York: Flatiron Books, 2015.

Hermann, Ned. "What Is the Function of the Various Brainwaves?" *Scientific American*, December 22, 1997. http://1ref.us/gv.

Hogan, Brenda, and Charles Young. *Introduction to Coping with Health Anxiety*. London: Constable and Robinson, 2007.

Klavon, Susan. "Beauty for Ashes: A Dedicated Owner's Journey Through-and Past-Her Dog's Mental Illness." *The Whole Dog Journal* 18, no. 8, (August 2015).

Kondo, Marie. *The Life Changing Magic of Tidying Up: The Japanese Art of Decluttering and Organizing*. Berkeley, CA: Ten Speed Press, 2014.

Maddock, Richard. "Panic Attacks as a Problem of pH." *Scientific American*, May 18, 2010. http://1ref.us/gw.

Marshall, Jacqueline. "The Impact of Solar Flares on the Human Mood and Psyche." *Communities Digital News*, September 15, 2014. http://1ref.us/gx.

McDougall, John. "Widespread Infection with Leukemia Virus from Meat and Milk." *The McDougall Newsletter* 3, no. 2 (February 2004).

Mercola, Joseph. "Extreme Endurance Exercise: If You Do This Type of Exercise You Could Be Damaging Your Heart." *Mercola.com* (blog), August 23, 2013. http://1ref.us/gy.

Mercola, Joseph. "Aspartame: By Far the Most Dangerous Substance Added to Most Foods Today." *Mercola.com* (blog), November 6, 2011. http://1ref.us/gz.

Nedley, Neil. *Nedley Depression & Anxiety Recovery Program Workbook*. Ardmore, OK: Nedley Publishing, 2015.

Neuroskeptic. "In the Brain, Acidity Means Anxiety." *discovermagazine.com* (blog), December 14, 2009. http://1ref.us/h0.

Newberg, Andrew. *The Spiritual Brain: Science and Religious Experience*. Chantilly, VA: The Great Courses, 2012.

Nikiforov, Yuri E., Raja R. Seethala, Giovanni Tallini, Zubair W. Baloch, Fulvio Basolo, Lester D. R. Thompson, Justine A. Barletta, Bruce M. Wenig, Abir Al Ghuzlan, Kennichi Kakudo, Thomas J. Giordano, Venancio A. Alves, Elham Khanafshar, Sylvia L. Asa, Adel K. El-Naggar, William E. Gooding, Steven P. Hodak, Ricardo V.

Lloyd, Guy Maytal, Ozgur Mete, Marina N. Nikiforova, Vania Nosé, Mauro Papotti, David N. Poller, Peter M. Sadow, Arthur S. Tischler, R. Michael Tuttle, Kathryn B. Wall, Virginia A. Livolsi, Gregory W. Randolph, and Ronald A. Ghossein. "Nomenclature Revision for Encapsulated Follicular Variant of Papillary Thyroid Carcinoma." *JAMA Oncology JAMA Oncol* 2, no. 8 (2016): 1023. doi:10.1001/jamaoncol.2016.0386.

Ortner, Nick. *The Tapping Solution: A Revolutionary System for Stress-Free Living*. Carlsbad, CA: Hay House, Inc., 2013.

Pollan, Michael. *In Defense of Food*. New York: Penguin Books, 2008.

Quinn, Dick. *Left For Dead*. Minneapolis, MN: R.F. Quinn Publishing Co., 2010.

Rankin, Lissa. *Mind Over Medicine: Scientific Proof That You Can Heal Yourself*. Carlsbad, CA: Hay House, Inc., 2013.

Schwartz, Jeffrey M., and Beverly Beyette. *Brainlock: Freeing Yourself from Obsessive-Compulsive Disorder*. New York, NY: Harper Collins, 1996.

Siegel, Robert Simon. *Six Seconds to True Calm Thriving Skills for 21st Century Living*. Santa Monica, CA: Little Sun Books, 1995.

Sims, Darren. *Conquering Health Anxiety How to Break Free from the Hypochondria Trap*. CreateSpace, 2014.

St. Amand, R. Paul, and Claudia Craig Marek. *What Your Doctor May Not Tell You About Fibromyalgia: The Revolutionary Treatment That Can Reverse the Disease*. New York, NY: Warner Wellness, 2006.

Stokowski, Laura A. "Alcohol and Cancer: Drink at Your Own Risk." *Medscape Nurses*, November 23, 2015. http://1ref.us/h1 (subscription required).

Straus, Howard, and Barbara Marinacci. *Dr. Max Gerson Healing the Hopeless*. Carmel, CA: Totality Books, 2009.

Taylor, Jill Bolte. *My Stroke of Insight: A Brain Scientist's Personal Journey*. New York, NY: Viking Penguin, 2008.

Trowbridge, John Parks, and Morton Walker. *The Yeast Syndrome How to Help Your Doctor Identify and Treat the Real Cause of Your Yeast-related Illness*. New York, NY: Bantam Books, 1986.

Wehrenberg, Margaret. *The 10 Best-Ever Anxiety Management Techniques Understanding How Your Brain Makes You Anxious & What You Can Do About It*. New York, NY: W.W. Norton & Company, 2008.

Young, Simon N., Scott E. Smith, Robert O. Pihl, and Frank R. Ervin. "Tryptophan Depletion Causes a Rapid Lowering of Mood in Normal Males." *Psychopharmacology* 87, no. 2 (1985): 173-77. doi:10.1007/bf00431803.

Zgourides, George D. *Stop Worrying About Your Health! How to Quit Obsessing About Symptoms and Feel Better Now* (2nd ed.). Raleigh, NC: Lulu Press, Inc., 2014.

Helpful Resources

http://1ref.us/h2 (Daily Strength)
http://1ref.us/h3 (No More Panic UK)
http://1ref.us/h4 (AnxietyUK)
http://1ref.us/h5 (Anxiety and Depression Association of America)

Index

A

Acetaldehyde 39, 130
Acidity 127
Alcohol 8, 19, 39, 40, 128
Amygdala 22
Anxiety disorders 10, 11, 65, 77
Arachidonic acid 45

B

Brain waves 113
Bravery 120
Breathing 35, 61

C

Caffeine 41, 51, 114
Clutter 113
Cortisol 24, 40

D

Dairy 47
Dancing 7
Depression 125, 127, 129
Discernment 66
Dogs 87
Dopamine 20, 40
Dread 90

E

Endorphins 21, 40
Endotoxins 45
Evans, Michael 122, 126
Exercise 59, 109, 127

F

Fasting 54, 55
Fat 51

Fearaholism 106
Fillmore, Myrtle 119

G

Gamma amino butyric acid
    (GABA) 19
Gerson therapy 49
Grains 52
Greger, Michael 18, 40, 42, 45, 50,
    52, 58, 74, 75, 120, 126
Guilt 100

H

Herbs 53
Histamine 36
Hydration 45, 51

I

IGF-1 47, 54
Images 26, 40, 54, 68, 87, 88, 91,
    104, 111
Intuition 21, 27, 69, 116, 119

K

Kluver-Bucy syndrome 23

L

Laughing 95, 98

M

Meditation 113
Melatonin 56, 57
Mercola, Joseph 54, 109, 127
Mindfulness 115

N

Nedley, Neil 20, 21, 110, 127
Neurotransmitters 18

Nightmares 57, 94
Nocebo 96
Norepinephrine 20, 40

O

Oxytocin 20, 111

P

Panic 8, 19, 20, 35, 36, 41, 43, 44,
    45, 61, 68, 72, 75, 81, 85, 102,
    114, 118
Phobia 107
Physicians 14
Pineal gland 56, 103
Placebo 96
Plan 91
Pollan, Michael 30, 127
Prayer 106, 115

Q

Quinn, Dick 53, 128

R

Rumi 110, 121

S

Safety behaviors 72, 73, 77, 78, 88,
    102, 106
Seasonal affective disorder 103
Secondary gain 79, 80
Serotonin 19, 20, 22, 106, 126
Sleep 55, 56, 57
Sun, little 126, 128

T

Tapping 117, 118, 127
Taylor, Jill Bolte 26, 128
Thinking errors 78, 85

Index

Thoreau, David Henry 116
Thought stopping 90
Thyroid 127
Tryptophan 57, 128

U

Uncertainty 102
Urbach-Wiethe disease 23

V

Vitamins 52

W

Wark, Chris 49

We invite you to view the complete
selection of titles we publish at:

www.TEACHServices.com

scan with your mobile
device to go directly
to our website

Please write or email us your praises, reactions, or
thoughts about this or any other book we publish at:

11 Quartermaster Circle
Fort Oglethorpe, GA 30742

Info@TEACHServices.com

TEACH Services, Inc., titles may be purchased in bulk for
educational, business, fund-raising, or sales promotional use.
For information, please e-mail:

BulkSales@TEACHServices.com

Finally if you are interested in seeing
your own book in print, please contact us at

publishing@TEACHServices.com

We would be happy to review your manuscript for free.

www.ingramcontent.com/pod-product-compliance
Lightning Source LLC
Chambersburg PA
CBHW070541170426
43200CB00011B/2510